JEFFERSON IN LOVE

JEFFERSON IN LOVE

The Love Letters Between
Thomas Jefferson &
Maria Cosway

EDITED BY JOHN P. KAMINSKI

MADISON HOUSE

Madison · 1999

LIBRARY OF CONGRESS CATALOGING-IN-PUBLICATION DATA

Jefferson, Thomas, 1743–1826.
Jefferson in love : love letters between Thomas Jefferson & Maria Cosway /
edited by John P. Kaminski. – 1st ed.
p.   cm.
Includes bibliographical references and index.
ISBN 0-945612-56-7 (alk. paper)
1. Jefferson, Thomas, 1743–1826 – Correspondence. 2. Presidents – United
States – Correspondence. 3. Diplomats – France – Paris – Correspondence.
4. Cosway, Maria Hadfield, 1759–1838 – Correspondence. 5. Jefferson, Thomas,
1743–1826 – Relations with women. 6. Love-letters – France – Paris. I. Cosway,
Maria Hadfield, 1759–1838. II. Kaminski, John P. III. Title.
E332.88.C67 1998   973.4'6'092 – dc21 [B]
98-45898 CIP

Typeset in Bell.
Designed by William Kasdorf.

Printed in the United States of America
on acid-free recycled paper.

Published by
Madison House Publishers, Inc.
P.O. Box 3100 · Madison, WI 53704

FIRST EDITION

For Steven & Lynn
and Susan & Bill

Contents

Preface

WHY EDIT A VOLUME OF LETTERS between Thomas Jefferson and Maria Cosway, an obscure Anglo-Italian artist? The correspondence chronicles no political, social or economic transformation; as strictly personal letters, they affected few besides their authors. What value does this correspondence have for us today?

Thomas Jefferson and Maria Cosway met by chance in 1786 and, within a fourteen-month span, they were in close proximity for less than two months on two separate occasions. During their first encounter, Jefferson and Cosway were together almost daily; during their second interlude, they saw each other infrequently. And yet, virtually every assessment of Jefferson's five-year European experience and every meaningful attempt to understand Jefferson-the-man dwell on the relationship cultivated with this beautiful, gracious and talented Continental woman. The reason for this interest is more than salacious. These letters provide the clearest window through which to view and assess Jefferson's personality. Just as he espied the Virginia countryside through the lens of his mountaintop home, so we can observe and discover Jefferson uniquely through these letters. No other extant letters give us such insight into the psyche of this enigmatic man. (Unfortunately Jefferson destroyed his correspondence with his wife Martha shortly after her untimely death.) His famous head-and-heart letter to Cosway clearly presents the contending forces in Jefferson's intellect and emotions.

Over and above the portal into Jefferson's inner soul, the letters are simply a beautifully-written exchange between two persons who felt passionately about each other. They make for good reading— particularly Jefferson's letters—from both a literary and a personal perspective. John Jay, Jefferson's diplomatic chief in New York, told the Marchioness de Lafayette in 1785 that it was "an old observation that ladies write better letters than gentlemen, and therefore, independent of other considerations, a correspondence between them is always so far on unequal terms." The "other independent consideration" in the Jefferson-Cosway correspondence was Jefferson himself—one of the greatest writers in the English language. Maria readily admitted that her letters were "sad scrawls" next to his eloquently crafted communications. The passion that Jefferson brought to this letter-writing merely enhanced their elegance.

There is also a sense of tragedy that looms over these letters. We know the outcome before reading even one of them. Jefferson and Cosway were star-crossed. They could never be together. As a widower, he was eligible;

she, however, was not. Divorce was impossible given Maria's strong Catholicism and Jefferson's public role. Jefferson could not stay permanently in Europe; Cosway (given her love of her Italian birthplace) could never abandon Europe. In their heart of hearts, they both knew that their relationship was forever restricted. They accepted that fact and drew pleasure from their limited relationship both in the brief time that they shared together and in the longer hours when their imaginations let them deepen their attachment.

For the first time, this volume brings together all of the romantic letters between Jefferson and Maria Cosway in one easy to read volume. Furthermore, the letters are fully translated and annotated for the first time. The volume stops in 1790, because that is when the romance ended. Although another thirteen letters between Jefferson and Cosway survive, these letters are clearly of a different nature. The affection and respect remain; the passion and romance vanish. Their lives changed without each other; they each sought new sanctuary—Jefferson in public service; Cosway in Italy apart from her husband and newborn daughter. A four-year lapse in corresponding provided the emotional break both needed.

JEFFERSON AND COSWAY HAD their idiosyncrasies in writing. Jefferson, for instance, seldom capitalized the first letter in a sentence and he often changed the spelling of certain words intentionally aiming at an Americanization of the English language (e.g., acknolege, knoledge). He almost always used the contraction "it's" for the possessive pronoun "its." Both he and Cosway used standard eighteenth-century abbreviations. Because these peculiarities tend merely to distract (not to inform) the twentieth-century reader, they have been altered to modern practice.

In her early correspondence, Cosway occasionally reverted to Italian. These passages have been translated and placed within curly brackets. Short phrases or individual words written in a foreign language (French, Italian or Latin) have been left in the text unchanged, and translations appear in the margin of the page. Jefferson usually signed his letters "Th: Jefferson" or "T. J."; Cosway usually signed hers "Maria Cosway" or "M. C." On occasion they left their letters unsigned, in which case their signatures have been supplied within brackets. The original manuscript letters have suffered damage over the years. Ellipses within brackets indicate that the text is illegible.

THE PUBLISHED WORKS useful in preparing this volume are cited in the bibliography. Two works deserve special mention. *The Papers of Thomas Jefferson* edited by

Julian P. Boyd and Helen Duprey Bullock's *My Head and My Heart: A Little History of Thomas Jefferson and Maria Cosway*. Richard Leffler and Greg Britton read the introduction and annotation and offered their usual excellent advice. My daughter-in-law Lynn Kaminski also read the introduction. Professor Domenico Sella assisted greatly in translating foreign text. Thanks are due also to my good friend and colleague John Catanzariti, from 1986 to 1998 the editor-in-chief of the Jefferson Papers at Princeton, who shared his knowledge about the Jefferson–Cosway correspondence with me. Peter Drummey and Virginia H. Smith of the Massachusetts Historical Society graciously assisted by sending me copies of the letters in the Society's Jefferson Collection.

This volume is dedicated to my son and daughter-in-law Steven and Lynn Kaminski and my sister and brother-in-law Susan and Bill Noble. They feel toward each other the love that Jefferson and Maria felt.

JEFFERSON IN LOVE

Introduction

AFTER TWO UNSUCCESSFUL YEARS as the war-time governor of Virginia in 1780 and 1781, the thirty-eight-year-old Thomas Jefferson left politics and returned home to his farm at Monticello convinced that he was ill suited for public service. Less than two years later, in early September 1782, Jefferson's beloved wife died and for several months he fell into what must have been a clinical depression. Wanting to alleviate his friend's anguish, James Madison, then serving in Congress, coaxed Jefferson back into public life by obtaining an appointment for him as one of America's five commissioners to negotiate a peace treaty with Great Britain. Jefferson accepted the assignment, but as he prepared to leave for Europe, news arrived that a preliminary treaty had been signed and Congress withdrew its commission.

The Virginia legislature then appointed Jefferson a delegate to Congress, where he soon became one of that body's most active members. The following year he accepted a two-year commission to join Benjamin Franklin and John Adams in Paris as an agent to negotiate commercial treaties with European countries. When Franklin resigned as U.S. ambassador to France, Congress elevated Jefferson to that post. Jefferson would remain abroad for more than five years. On his return to America in November 1789—which he expected to be only a temporary stay before returning to his French post—he found that President George Washington had appointed him the first Secretary of State under the new federal Constitution. With some trepidation, Jefferson accepted the appointment and canceled his return plans for Paris.

LEAVING HIS TWO YOUNGER daughters with his sister, Jefferson and his twelve-year-old daughter Martha (Patsy) set sail from Boston for Paris on July 5, 1784. The speedy 19-day Atlantic voyage was "as favorable as could have been asked in every possible circumstance." Patsy described it as "a lovely passage" in a beautiful new ship that had made only one previous voyage. There were but six passengers aboard the *Ceres*, "all of whom papa knew, and a fine sun shined all the way, with the sea . . . as calm as a river." After a stay of four days in England to allow Patsy to recover from a fever, Jefferson and his daughter crossed the stormy English Channel, and after a difficult thirteen-hour voyage they landed at Havre de Grace at the mouth of the Seine. Arriving at harvest time, their trip to Paris via "a most pleasing road" along the Seine provided a picturesque view of the fertile, well cultivated, and elegantly improved countryside dotted with old churches bejeweled with beautiful stained glass windows. Less pleasant were the swarms of beggars who surrounded them at every rest stop.

The Jeffersons arrived in Paris on August 6. To transform their rustic American appearance, Patsy got a new wardrobe more suited for urban life and Jefferson bought a sword and belt, buckles, knee breeches, lace ruffles, embroidered waistcoats, and silk stockings. When Jefferson called on French Foreign Minister Vergennes, the count asked whether he had come to replace "le Docteur Franklin." Jefferson responded, "No one can *replace* him, sir. I am only his *successor.*"

Jefferson arranged for Patsy to be boarded at the Abbaye Royale de Panthémont, the most exclusive convent-school in Paris. Half of the sixty girls at the convent were Protestants; three were princesses of royal blood. Religion was never part of the curriculum: lay professionals did the teaching and the nuns were assigned the menial duties. Soon Patsy, called by her classmates "Jeffy," was speaking "French as easily as English," but the language barrier continued a serious obstacle for her father. Fortunately Jefferson could draw on a number of American friends in Paris. Franklin and John and Abigail Adams were regular companions, and soon Jefferson's protégé William Short would arrive. Fluent in French, Short would become

Jefferson's personal secretary throughout the latter's ambassadorial tenure.

Jefferson suffered during his first winter abroad. "A seasoning as they call it is the lot of most strangers: and none I believe have experienced a more severe one than myself. The air is extremely damp, and the waters very unwholesome." Added to his physical ailments, the Marquis de Lafayette brought letters from America with the heartbreaking news that Jefferson's two-and-a-half-year-old daughter Lucy Elizabeth had died. For most of the winter the devastated father remained confined. But finally the sun, Jefferson's "almighty physician," reappeared and with it his health and spirits. Soon he was back to his usual regimen, walking four to five miles daily through the tree-lined paths of the Bois de Boulogne.

In mid-May 1785 the Adams family left Paris for London, leaving Jefferson, in his own words, "in the dumps." Two months later Benjamin Franklin set off for America. Jefferson formally presented his credentials as ambassador to Louis XVI on May 17. He rented new quarters at the Hôtel de Langeac, a mansion built for a mistress of a minister of Louis XV, at the Grille de Chaillot on the corner of the Champs-Élysées and the Rue Neuve de Barry. The rent was too expensive, but the spacious building provided the necessary accommodations for Jefferson and his staff and provided the appropriate dignity for the young republic. Jefferson also had started to appreciate Europe's cultural amenities. "I enjoy their architecture, sculpture, painting, music. . . . It is in these arts they shine. The last of them particularly is an enjoyment."

In March 1786 John Adams asked Jefferson to visit London to conclude treaty negotiations with the Portuguese ambassador and with an unofficial diplomatic agent from Tripoli. Congress' commissions to Adams, Jefferson, and Franklin required at least two of the agents to agree to any treaty. Because Franklin had returned to America and because little time remained on their commissions, both American diplomats were eager to conclude successful negotiations. They also looked forward to seeing each other again. Unfortunately, however, negotiations collapsed, and Jefferson set off for Paris on April 26.

In early August 1786, the artist John Trumbull arrived in Paris. Son of a former governor of Connecticut and an aide-de-camp to George Washington during the early part of the Revolution, Trumbull had left the army and come to Europe to study painting. Jefferson had met Trumbull four months earlier in London and described him as "a young painter of great and increasing

reputation." Trumbull accepted Jefferson's invitation to
visit Paris and be his house guest. Through Trumbull's
association, Jefferson's life was to change dramatically.

Sometime in August Jefferson and Trumbull arranged to visit the Halle aux Bléds, Paris' magnificent
indoor, domed marketplace. While imagining a rep-
lica constructed in Richmond, the new capital of Virginia, Jefferson caught sight of a stunningly beautiful
woman. He couldn't take his eyes off of her. Noticing
his friend's distraction, Trumbull introduced Jefferson
to Maria Cosway—and to her husband. Richard and
Maria Cosway, two of Trumbull's artist friends from
London, had come to Paris for Richard to paint the
debaucherous Duchess of Polignac and the Duchess
d'Orléans and her children. The party of four continued together throughout the afternoon. They all canceled evening engagements to stay together longer.
In a "lying message," Jefferson told the Duchess
d'Anville that he would be unable to keep their dinner
engagement because important diplomatic dispatches
had arrived that needed his immediate attention. The
four new friends dined at the village of St. Cloud, then
went on to Ruggieri's, a cabaret-style garden restaurant where they listened to musical pieces from an orchestra and watched a dazzling fireworks display. Then
on to hear Johann and Julie Krumpholtz, the most re-

nowned harpists on the Continent. The evening raced by and all too soon Jefferson and Trumbull bade the Cosways good night.

For the next few days, the four friends continued their sightseeing together. Soon, however, Trumbull left for Germany and Richard Cosway busied himself with his painting. Day after day, Thomas and Maria wended their way throughout the châteaus and gardens of the Parisian countryside. For six weeks they spent days and half days together. Jefferson had fallen in love, something he had promised himself he would never do again after his wife's death. But Cosway was unlike any other woman he had ever known. He couldn't help himself; he was irresistibly drawn to her—smitten with what he called a "generous spasm of the heart."

MARIA LOUISA CATHERINE CECELIA HADFIELD was born in 1759 near Florence, Italy, of English parents. Her father owned a hotel that catered to English travelers visiting Italy. Four of Maria's six siblings were killed tragically by a deranged nurse, who intended to make little Maria her next victim. The diabolical scheme was discovered just in time to save Maria. Under the patronage of the Duke and Duchess of Tuscany, the dis-

tressed child was placed in a convent, where her musical and artistic talents developed. There she learned
to play the harp and the harpsichord quite well. Although she considered Italian to be her native tongue,
she became fluent in five or six languages, which she
often mixed as she spoke. Maria studied painting with
several masters, becoming expert at both landscapes
and miniature portraits. Several of her paintings were
displayed at the Academy of Fine Arts in Florence to
which she was elected at the age of nineteen.

When her father died in 1778, Maria decided to become a nun. Her mother, realizing that only Maria could
provide for the family by entering into an advantageous
marriage, convinced her dutiful daughter to accompany
her to London. Here, Maria became the protégé of Angelica Kaufmann, the foremost female painter on the
Continent. Through Kaufmann, the doors of the artistic
community opened. Maria's portrait of the Duchess of
Devonshire and various exhibitions of her work brought
acclaim. Soon eligible suitors called on Maria. She was
attracted to William Parsons, but the thirty-five-year-
old music professor did not satisfy her mother and Angelica. Instead, they preferred Richard Cosway, a talented
and socially prominent artist. The two were married in
January 1781.

Nearly twice Maria's age, Cosway was the most

prominent painter of miniatures in England. The lecherous Prince of Wales was his patron; and, despite his obvious talent, Cosway had an unsavory reputation that included painting pornographic miniatures on snuff boxes. A short, foppish man, rumors abounded about his sexual escapades both before and after his marriage, both with women as well as men—perhaps even with the Prince of Wales. Cosway was satirized as the man with the monkey face—a macaroni.

Richard Cosway used his beautiful, young wife to the fullest advantage. He kept her "retired" for a year until she became acquainted with society and with English culture. Once she had been sufficiently assimilated, the Cosways regularly entertained the *haut monde* in their fabulously decorated mansion on Pall Mall. Maria would sing and play the harp and harpsichord, often to music she composed herself. The wealthiest and socially most prominent would visit their salon, mornings and evenings, where Maria would charm the men. Hoping to see her again, they would readily engage Richard Cosway to paint them. Cosway, jealous of his wife's artistic talent, restricted her to painting landscapes and portraits of her friends. Never did he allow her to paint professionally, and she focused on her music and engraving.

As a native of the Florentine countryside, Maria

hated London. The damp, dreary foggy climate deepened her natural melancholia. The streets were filthy, and black smoke belched out from hundreds of factories. Maria dreamed of escape. When the opportunity to vacation in Paris presented itself, Maria jumped at it. She loved Paris, and, in the handsome, intelligent, and charming American diplomat, she found the perfect man to paint into her exquisite new world. For six weeks she was happy.

From mid-August through mid-September 1786, Jefferson and Cosway enjoyed each other's company almost daily. To him, Maria was the exemplary woman —twenty-seven years old, with a slim, graceful figure, curly golden hair that cascaded from the enormous heights of her coiffure to below her shoulders, smooth skin, large violet-blue eyes, saucy lips, a melodic Italian-accented voice, blithe spirit, and fashionable dress. Her music and art drew him even closer. Moreover, she had a way of making him feel comfortable—with her and with himself. They could talk for hours, but never about politics—a subject Jefferson felt women should eschew. According to Jefferson, Cosway possessed "qualities and accomplishments, belonging to her sex, which might form a chapter apart for her: such as music, modesty, beauty, and that softness of disposition which is the ornament of her sex and charm of ours."

On one of their outings in mid-September, Jefferson's boyish enthusiasm went awry. As the enraptured paramour attempted to leap over a hedge he fell and dislocated or fractured his right wrist. Exactly how this accident occurred is uncertain. Jefferson wrote that an explanation "would be a long story for the left [hand] to tell. It was by one of those follies from which good cannot come, but ill may." The excruciating pain remained for weeks. To add to his anguish, Mr. Cosway finished his painting and, perhaps sensing that Jefferson and Maria had become too close, announced that he and his wife would leave for a month-long tour of Antwerp, Flanders, and northern France, and then return to London. Both Jefferson and Maria dreaded the parting.

Their last soiree occurred on the day before her expected departure. The jostling of the carriage seriously aggravated his injury. Distressed, Thomas wrote Maria the following morning that he would be unable to accompany her to St. Denis from which the Cosways would take a carriage to Antwerp. He had spent a sleepless night and had called for the surgeon to examine his throbbing wrist. Maria responded immediately. She blamed herself for his renewed pain. She should have insisted that he stay home, but she could not resist one more time having "the pleasure of your company." She told him that she would always "remember the charming days we have past together"; she would "long for next spring" when she hoped to return to Paris and they would be together again.

Despite his pain, Jefferson forced himself to accompany the Cosways to St. Denis. After assisting Maria into her carriage, he walked away "more dead than alive." Later that night, seated by his fireside, "solitary and sad," he composed an elegant love letter to his Maria in the form of a dialogue between his head and his heart. Over the course of several days, he refined the dialogue, and then finally on October 12, he wrote out the final copy with his left hand. Fortunately for posterity, Jefferson had only recently started to use a portable press-copy machine that he had seen on his trip to London. Without such a copying device, the head-and-heart letter, as well as most of Jefferson's other letters to Maria, would never have been preserved.

The head-and-heart letter is one of the rare times that Jefferson laid bare his innermost thoughts. We see Jefferson's intellect and emotions jousting. His heart admitted that with Cosway's absence he was "indeed the most wretched of all earthly beings. Overwhelmed with grief, every fiber of my frame distended beyond its natural powers to bear." His head berated his heart for being so pained by the loss of Maria. The heart begged for mercy. "This is no moment to upbraid my foibles. I am rent into fragments by the force of my grief! If you have any balm, pour it into my wounds." The head would not relent. The heart never listened to the head during moments of triumph; perhaps while suffering from its follies, the heart would receive the head's medicine and learn a valuable lesson.

The head recollected the events of the day when Thomas first met Maria. At the end of that day it seemed to the heart as if he had known Maria a month. The heart recalled other days when he and Maria were alone—the day at the terrace and gardens of St. Germains was perhaps, the heart queried, "a little too warm, I think, was not it?" "Thou art," exclaimed the head, "the most incorrigible of all the beings that ever sinned!" Such relationships are more painful than death. With death, our sufferings end; with separations from those you love, the pain merely begins.

The head warned against friends made so easily and so deeply. "Consider what advantages it presents, and to what inconveniences it may expose you. Do not bite at the bait of pleasure till you know there is no hook beneath it. The art of life is the art of avoiding pain." The heart saw things differently. "Friendship is precious." Maria had brought him a new zest for living. Each site they visited "wore its liveliest hue" because of her presence. "They were pleasing, because she seemed pleased. Alone, the scene would have been dull and insipid: the participation of it with her gave it relish." Happiness, the heart explained, is not merely the absence of pain. "We have no rose without its thorn; no pleasure without alloy." Yes, the heart admitted "I feel more fit for death than life. But when I look back on the pleasures of which it is the consequence, I am conscious they were worth the price I am paying."

Leaving the dialogue, Thomas told Maria that his health was good, except for his wrist which was mending slowly, "and my mind which mends not at all, but broods constantly over your departure." A bit embarrassed by the length of his letter, Jefferson wanted Cosway to read only one-sixth of it each day. He knew quite well, however, she would be unable to set the letter down once she started reading it. Along with his head-and-heart letter, Jefferson sent Maria the sheet music *Jours heureux!* "Happy Days!," an aria from Sacchini's opera *Daranus*, which Thomas and Maria attended together two days before she departed for Antwerp. He had promised to send her the music; he hoped she would "sing it with feeling"; he beseeched her to return to Paris and bring with her their happy days.

When Cosway arrived in London, Jefferson's correspondence awaited her. She was overwhelmed with the dialogue. Her heart, she said, was mute. "Whatever I may say will appear trifling." She could spend "an hour to consider every word, to every sentence [she] could write a volume." She apologized to Jefferson for violating his instructions about reading the letter piecemeal—she "could not resist the desire to read it at once, even at the cost of committing an act of disobedience. Forgive me," she pleaded, "the crime merits it."

Cosway eagerly awaited new letters from her American friend, but they never arrived soon enough to satisfy her. She pleaded with him to make his letters shorter but more frequent. She told Jefferson that she no longer had patience to wait.

Jefferson apologized for his delay in writing. His busy schedule, sore wrist, and unwillingness to impose long letters on Maria were all used to justify his sporadic writing. Above all else, he needed to wait for a safe conveyance to London by private carrier, because the French and British post offices always opened his mail. He hated the idea that "the breathings of a pure affection would be profaned by the eye of a commis of the poste." When he did use the regular mail, he often disguised his seal and signature. He instructed Cosway to address her letters to him in the care of

Ferdinand Grand, a Swiss-born, Parisian banker. He assured Cosway that he was "never happier than when I commit myself into dialogue with you, tho' it be but in imagination." Despite his tardiness in writing, he encouraged Maria to "Write to me often. Write affectionately, and freely, as I do to you. Say many kind things, and say them without reserve. They will be food for my soul."

Repeatedly Thomas told Maria of his desire to be with her. When Madame de Corny, one of Jefferson and Cosway's "little coterie," traveled to London, Jefferson wished that "she could put me into her pocket, when she goes, or you, when she comes back." He remembered the history of Fortunatus who "had a cap of such virtues that when he put it on his head, and wished himself anywhere, he was there." Jefferson had long wished for such a cap. "Yet if I had it, I question if I should use it but once. I should wish myself with you, and not wish myself away again." While waiting for the cap, Thomas told Maria, "I am always thinking of you. If I cannot be with you in reality, I will in imagination." He wondered when she would return to Paris. He did not want to be told that she would never return. "I had rather be deceived, than live without hope. It is so sweet! It makes us ride so smoothly over the roughnesses of life. When clambering a mountain, we always hope the hill we are on is the last. But it is the next, and the next, and still the next." When Maria did return to Paris, Jefferson was determined "not to admit the idea that we are ever to part again." In saying good-by, he asked Maria to "Place me in your breast with those who you love most: and comfort me with your letters.".

Even when Cosway received letters from Jefferson, she was disappointed because they were never as long as his head-and-heart letter. She had become "an enfant gatée," a spoiled child. She realized, however, that her complaints would only "tease you to a hatred towards me, notwithstanding your partiality you have had for me till now." Later Maria apologized for her complaints. The shortness of his letters appeared "only on the first glance in the paper, but when I read, you seem to say so much in few words that I forget the little number of the syllables for the beauty of the expressions and elegant style." Thomas responded by always encouraging Maria to write letters that were "lengthy, warm, and flowing from the heart."

On August 28, 1787, Cosway returned to Paris alone. A guest in the house of the beautiful Franco-Polish Princess Aleskandra Lubomirska, the lengthy distance from Jefferson's residence made it difficult for the two friends to escape spontaneously to the countryside. Cosway was eager to be with Jefferson again but she was also occupied with establishing her own Parisian salon to which she could return regularly. The *haut monde* regularly attended her apartment and Jefferson resented sharing her with a crowd of admirers. Neither Cosway nor Jefferson would express their feelings openly. Both stubbornly waited for the other to make the first overture. Maria wanted Thomas to assert himself and sweep her off on another romantic itinerary. He, feeling abandoned, kept silent and stayed away. On several occasions they attempted visits only to find the other not at home.

Jefferson explained the unhappy situation to John Trumbull. "A fatality has attended my wishes, and her and my endeavors to see one another more since she has been here. From the mere effect of chance, she has happened to be from home several times when I have called on her, and I, when she has called on me. I hope for better luck hereafter." Only occasionally did they repeat their pleasant outings of the previous year. The cooler weather of late autumn seemed also to dampen their spirits. Only as Maria prepared to return to London did Jefferson realize his lost opportunity. He hosted a gala going-away dinner for Maria. Maria could not understand. "Why will you make such a great dinner?" she asked him. Sadly, she lamented their lost opportunities. "If my inclination had been your law I should have had the pleasure of seeing you more than I have. I have felt the *loss* with displeasure." Jefferson, however, felt unable to demand her individual attention and company. Only after she returned to London did he write excusing his lack of assertiveness. "It was not my fault, unless it be a fault to love my friends so dearly as to wish to enjoy their company in the only way it yields enjoyment, that is, en petit comité." Affectingly, he complained: "You make everybody love you. You are sought and surrounded therefore by all. Your mere domestic cortege was so numerous, *et si imposante* [and so imposing], that one could not approach you quite at their ease. Nor could you so unpremeditately mount into the phaeton and hie away to the Bois de Boulogne, St. Cloud, Marly, St. Germains etc. Add to this the distance at which you were placed from me." He hoped her next visit to Paris would be different. "When you come again, you must be nearer, and move more extempore."

On December 7, 1787, the night before her departure from Paris, Cosway and Jefferson met for the last time. She invited him to breakfast the following morning and he was to accompany her part way to Calais, but she left before he arrived at the appointed time. She explained herself in a brief note penned the preceding evening. "To bid you adieu once is sufficiently painful, for I leave you with very melancholy ideas." After arriving in London, she again apologized for her hasty departure. "I could not bear to take leave any more. I was confused and distracted, you must have thought me so when you saw me in the evening." Jefferson did not write to Cosway for two months. "I went to breakfast with you according to promise, and you had gone off at 5 o'clock in the morning. This spared me indeed the pain of parting, but it deprives me of the comfort of recollecting that pain." He again excused his failure to write because of the lack of a private conveyance and asked her to "think of me often and warmly, as I do of you."

In early March 1788, mutual friends returned to London from Paris with no letter for Maria. She waited to compose herself, but soon wrote to Jefferson "still *angry*." Worried that Jefferson was slipping away, she asked if he would allow John Trumbull to make a miniature portrait from the life-portrait Trumbull had recently painted in Paris of Jefferson and the Declaration of Independence. Trumbull wrote Jefferson sending Cosway's love. "She is angry," Trumbull said, "yet she teases me every day for a copy of your little portrait, that she may scold *it* no doubt." Jefferson received Cosway's angry letter on April

23, 1788, when he arrived back from a trip to Amsterdam and the Rhineland. He did not believe he was in arrears in his correspondence with her before he had left Paris. "In affection," he wrote, "I am sure you were greatly my debtor." His desire for Maria was perhaps at its peak. He told her about his travels. About how he preferred the paintings of Adriaen Van der Werff exhibited in Dusseldorf to those of Reubens. The latter's voluptuously sensuous "old faded red things" could not compare with the former's picture of the beautiful Hagar being brought by the barren, aged Sarah to her old husband's bed. It was easy for Jefferson to imagine himself as Abraham and Maria as Hagar. He called it "delicious." At Heidelberg he vicariously led her hand in hand through the gardens. At Strasbourg he confessed that he tried to write but could only think of Laurence Sterne's story of the stranger's nose. All he would have been able to do would have been to elaborate upon noses. (Unbeknownst to Maria, Sterne's story set in Strasbourg was a not so subtle satire about the traveler's enlarged penis held inviolate for his lost lover.) Thomas asked Maria to write him "soft testimonials" of her love; letters "teeming with affection; such as I feel for you." Maria responded harshly. How could he lead her by the hand through Europe and then "not find one word to write, *but on Noses?* No, this I cannot put up with, it is too bad." Maria's limited knowledge of English literature prevented her from appreciating Jefferson's erotic allusion.

The lovers longed to be together, but Maria could not promise another visit to Paris. "I am afraid to question My Lord and Master on this subject." Her husband might refuse to let her go. She invited Jefferson to London. "We should go to see many beautiful villas, enjoy all the best England can afford and make the rest up with our own society; we shall not have a numerous cortege, I promise to make myself and my society according to your own wish."

Three months lapsed before Jefferson would write again. Cosway prodded him with three more angry letters, signing the last "Maria Cosway in waiting." He finally had enough free time to write his friends, "and with none do I converse more fondly than with my good Maria." He had heard that she was becoming more reclusive. He liked the idea. "A great deal of love given to a few, is better than a little to many." He asked that she send him "a little visiting card" with a crayon drawing by which he could remember her. He would have it engraved on his visiting card "that our names may be together if our persons cannot. Adieu, my dear friend, love me much, and love me always."

Three days later he wrote again explaining that the rush of business had kept him from writing before. He told her he was "incapable of forgetting or neglecting" her. He felt sure that he thought of her more than she of him. "Of this I have no right to complain, nor do I complain. You esteem me as much as I deserve. If I love you more, it is because you deserve more." He assured her that "of voluntary faults to you I can never be guilty, and you are too good not to pardon the involuntary. Chide me then no more."

Cosway was overjoyed to receive the two letters. Her anger at Jefferson's tardiness was merely a manifestation of how much she cared for him. She always measured the distance from her friends, not by miles but by time. She was honored that he should request a drawing from her. She would gladly comply, hoping that it would hang "in the room you inhabit most" so that the artist would "be recalled to your remembrance as often as possible."

Cosway asked Jefferson if the rumor she had heard was true—was Jefferson going back to America soon? If so, she pleaded with him to come to England first. "It is but a little journey for so much pleasure you will procure us." She even suggested that a trip to Italy might be possible in 1789; she hoped Jefferson would join her. "Can you resist this proposition!" In a post-

script she happily announced that Trumbull had finally given her a miniature portrait. "Wish me joy for
I possess your picture."

Jefferson immediately answered Cosway's letter to
show her that "there is nothing nearer my heart than
to meet all the testimonies of your esteem." He lamented "I am going to America, and you to Italy. The
one or the other of us goes the wrong way, for the way
will ever be wrong which leads us farther apart." His
daughters needed to return to America. Patsy had announced her intention to convert to Catholicism. Immediately he withdrew her from the convent school
and planned her return to Virginia. But he would come
back to Europe within nine months. He had no idea
how long he would then remain in Paris. In perhaps
an oblique invitation, he suggested that "it would certainly be the longer had I a single friend here like yourself." Better yet, Maria should visit him in America.
He would "find excuses for being sometimes of your
parties." In his next letter, Thomas told Maria he was
presuming that she would join him in America. "We
are apt to believe what we wish." He would show her
the new world. Acknowledging, however, that this
might never happen, "let us be together in spirit. Preserve for me always a little corner in your affection in
exchange for the spacious part you occupy in mine."

Maria thanked him for the invitation but she could not accept. She would certainly be with him in spirit and "walk thro' the beautiful scenes you will describe to me by letter." But before he left Europe, again she pleaded with him to visit her in London.

As Jefferson awaited his official leave of absence, he wrote what he thought would be his final good-byes in Europe. He would think of her while sailing across the Atlantic. "When wafting on the bosom of the ocean I shall pray it to be as calm and smooth as yours to me. . . . Adieu, my very dear friend. Be our affections unchangeable, and if our little history is to last beyond the grave, be the longest chapter in it that which shall record their purity, warmth and duration."

Cosway received this letter thinking that Jefferson might already be on his way to America. She told him "I did long most excessively for a letter from you." She reveled in their correspondence. "I wish to converse longer with you. But when I read your letters they are so well wrote, so full of a thousand pretty things that it is not possible for me to answer such charming letters. I could say many things if my pen could write exactly my sentiments and feelings, but my letters must appear sad scrawls to you." Expecting to leave at a moment's notice, Jefferson sent his final farewells from Paris. He asked her to preserve her affection for him; it would "comfort me in going, and encourage me returning." He hoped to see her in Paris in May 1790. As Jefferson waited in England for the vessel to take him back to Virginia, Maria wrote him. She was ill, otherwise she would have come to see him. Sensing she might never see him again, she asked him to think of her sometimes. He looked forward to seeing her in Paris in the spring—in April "with the first swallow." "Remember me," he ended, "and love me."

On October 22, 1789, Jefferson and his daughters embarked from Cowes on the Isle of Wight, aboard the *Clermont*. A month later they arrived at Norfolk, Virginia. Another month found them at Monticello. Unexpectedly, he received official word from President Washington asking him to serve as secretary of state. Although pulled by the twin magnets of Monticello and Paris, Jefferson acceded to Washington's wishes and, after a short stay at home, left for New York. He would serve in the cabinet for four years.

After six months of silence, Cosway finally wrote to Jefferson. "I fear my dear friend has forgot me." She had heard about his appointment and understood why he was unable to write. She hoped that he would speak of her to their mutual friend John Trumbull. "I shall be happy to have my name breathed up by the delightful air of your country." Her letter was ecstasy to him. It gave him "a foretaste of the sensations we are to feel in the next world, on the arrival of any new-comer from the circle of friends we have left behind." He longed to see her, but they were "divided now by a wide sea." He again invited her to come to America. While waiting for her, he bid adieu and ended, "je vous aimerai toujours," I will always love you.

Jefferson and Cosway would exchange another dozen letters, but both knew they would never see each other again. Embroiled in national politics, never again would Jefferson travel abroad. Maria, who later told Jefferson she would travel to "the furthest part of Europe" to be with him, found it impossible to risk a transatlantic voyage. Furthermore, Jefferson had heard that Cosway was expecting her first child. She was no longer free to be with him.

Maria had a baby girl in early 1790, Louisa Paolina Angelica. By September she left the child, her husband, and her adopted country and returned to Italy accompanied by Luigi Marchesi, the noted castrato. Some reports indicated that illness and melancholy forced her to leave dreary London for the recuperative climes of her native land. Other reports suggested she needed to escape from her carousing husband. In any event, she stayed away for four years. While residing in a convent in Genoa, she heard of her husband's illness and returned to London. She nursed him back to health; but Richard, at his professional peak, became more eccentric and experimented with exotic religions and hallucinogens.

Shortly after returning to London, Maria spoke with John Trumbull and Angelica Church; both told her that Jefferson had asked about her in his recent correspondence. In November 1794, Maria wrote her old friend that "I am come home to England, and have the great pleasure to find I am not forgotten by Mr. Jefferson, tis impossible to express my happiness, the less I say the better. I am sure what I don't say will be added by a Heart who can conceive and interpret sentiments of a feeling and grateful heart." She told him that her antipathy for London's climate continued, especially after her long stay in beautiful Genoa, though the pleasure of the good society and amiable friends make in great measure a recompense." She often thought of America and wished she could make the journey.

Cosway told Jefferson about her daughter. "She shows natural talent and a good soft disposition." Maria had given up her own painting and music for the moment, and enjoyed instructing her daughter. But, what about Mr. Jefferson. She "supposed he was by now *un gran Papa!*"

Jefferson responded to Cosway in September 1795. He told her that he was "retired to my home in the full enjoyment of my farm, my family and my books. . . . I am eating the peaches, grapes and figs of my own garden and I only wish I could eat them in your native country, gathered on the spot and in your good company." He wondered how she could have left Italy again "for the smoke and rain of London. However," he told her, "you have the power of making fair weather wherever you go." He imagined a trip with her to Italy. They would first stop in France and then go on to the Riviera of Genoa where "together" they would see "many romantic scenes." The rest of the journey, he said, they should leave "to imagination.—in truth, whenever I think of you, I am hurried off on the wings of imagination into regions where fancy submits all things to our will." He ended his letter with regret for "the distance which separates us and will not permit myself to believe we are no more to meet till you meet me where time and distance are nothing."

How happy Cosway was to have "the long wished pleasure of receiving a letter" from Jefferson. She was pleased that he had retired to Monticello "from the busling world. . . . What would I give," she wrote, "to surprise you on your Monticello!" Although that was impossible, she reminded Jefferson that she had his picture painted by Trumbull "on the side of my chimney always before me." She regretted, however, "that perhaps never can I see the Original." His "letters t'would be some compensation, but to be deprived of both is too much."

For the next couple of years, Cosway devoted most of her attention to her daughter, who, from several fine portraits painted by her father, appears to have looked much like Maria. Richard Cosway left his wife and daughter and went on a six-month "sketching trip" with Mary Moser, a talented painter herself. Richard Cosway kept a journal which lasciviously described the journey complete with many invidious comparisons between Moser and Maria. Maria, aware of the adulterous relationship between her husband and Moser, seems to have accepted it with no recriminations. Her life was now totally entwined with her daughter. Tragically, however, the child died at the age of six on August 6, 1796, leaving Maria deeply depressed.

After months of seclusion, she buried much of her grief in her art, exhibiting both paintings and engravings at the Royal Academy. She traveled to France and in early 1802 announced an amazingly ambitious project in which she would prepare engravings of all the paintings in the Louvre, along "with an historical account of each picture, and such authentic anecdotes of the artists, as may be new and interesting."

While in Paris, Cosway wrote Jefferson that every day she remembered "our first interview, the pleasing days we passed together." She so wanted him to return to Paris. He responded with warm memories of their "first interview [that] has produced an attachment which has never been diminished."

As the French Revolution exploded again into a global conflagration, French authorities stopped her work at the Louvre. Unable because of the war to get a passport to return to London, she moved to Lyons, where in 1803, at the request of the archbishop and with the approval of her husband, she founded "a college for young ladies." In October 1805 she wrote to Jefferson that she had "the consolation of being Mother of 60 children. Nothing is more interesting than rendering oneself useful to our fellow creatures, and what better way than that of making their education," a sentiment Jefferson must have shared.

When a change in the French government suspended the operation of the school at Lyons, Cosway traveled to her sister's in Milan. The Duke of Lodi invited her to found a school modelled on the one at Lyons and offered to provide a handsome villa for the site. In 1812 the college began. Maria ran the school with the understanding that she would return to London if needed by her husband. Such was the case when he suffered two paralytic strokes. While nursing her husband in London, she wrote to Jefferson in April 1819 after a silence of almost fourteen years. She remembered and valued their relationship so many years ago. "To the length of silence, I draw a curtain. Remembrance must be *ever grace*." She had often read about him in newspapers. "My humble situation," she said, "could never bring to you any public information of me, and I little trust on private ones being built on *Truth*." Her travels to the Continent were required by "bad health or other particular private melancholy motives, but on any sudden information of Mr. C's bad health, I hastened home to see him."

Cosway told Jefferson about her two schools that gave her so much fulfillment. "Who would have imagined, I should have taken up this line? It has afforded me satisfaction unfelt before; after having been deprived of my own child." But now, on leave from Lodi, she tended to her broken husband. "Happy in self gratification of doing my duty, with no other consolation." She remembered Jefferson's head-and-heart letter written thirty-five years earlier: "In your Dialogue your head would tell me, '*that is enough*,' your heart perhaps will understand, I might wish *for more*. God's will be done."

Jefferson responded a year and a half later. Two years of "prostrate health" and a stiffened right wrist from the old Parisian injury provided his only excuses for so belated a response to her "cherished letter." He rejoiced in her health, for he believed she must be in good health because she had not indicated otherwise. He praised her for being "so usefully and pleasingly occupied in preparing the minds of others to enjoy the blessings you have yourself derived from the same source, a cultivated mind." He told her about his twelve grandchildren and six great grandchildren amongst whom he lived "like a patriarch of old." Sorrowfully, he remembered their Parisian coterie—"dead, diseased, and dispersed." He was tired and felt that the end for him was near. "Mine is the next turn, and I shall meet it with good will; for after one's friends are all gone before them, and our faculties leaving us too, one by one, why wish to linger in mere vegetation? as a solitary trunk in a desolate field, from which all its former companions have disappeared." He hoped and expected that she had many healthy, happy, and productive years ahead of her. He was seventy-eight, she was sixty-two. But he looked forward to the time when "we shall meet again" in happiness in the world after death.

On July 4, 1821, at the age of eighty, Richard Cosway died from a stroke. Maria had always been aware of her husband's foibles, but his talent always seemed to balance out things for her. A week and a half after the death, she wrote Jefferson a letter edged in black. "I have been left a *widow*." She looked forward to returning to Lodi and only wished that *"Monticello* was not *so far!"* She would visit him on his charming little mountain; "but it is impossible."

On October 24, 1822, Jefferson wrote his last letter to Cosway. He was pleased that she would be financially solvent after her husband's death. Her life style would also improve when she moved "from the eternal clouds and rains of England to the genial sun and bright skies of Lodi." He relished the idea that they would both end their lives promoting education: "You retire to your college of Lodi and nourish the natural benevolence of your excellent heart by communicating your own virtues to the young of your sex who may hereafter load with blessings the memory of her to whom they will owe so much. I am laying the foundation of an University in my native state." He sensed that this might be his final letter as he hoped that her "days may pass in peace, in health and comfort." Maria, in turn, congratulated Jefferson on his university. "The work is worthy of you and you are worthy of such enjoyment." In her final letter to Jefferson, Cosway told of how she had her salon in Lodi painted with the four

parts of the world with the most distinguished objects represented in them. For North America, she had
Washington, D.C., painted in, but "left a hill barren"
upon which she hoped to paint Monticello and the new
Virginia university.

Jefferson died on July 4, 1826. Maria Cosway would
outlive him by almost twelve years. In 1830 she purchased the college's villa from the heirs of the Duke of
Lodi, and she settled a large endowment on the school.
She attached the buildings to the church of Santa Maria
della Grazie. Four years later Emperor Francis I of
Austria visited the college and made Maria a baroness
for her good deeds. Another four years passed, and
Maria Cosway died at the college on January 5, 1838,
much beloved and admired by her students. None, however, loved her more than had Thomas Jefferson.

JEFFERSON'S RELATIONSHIP WITH Cosway was unique in
his life, and historians have long disagreed about it.
Some have attacked Cosway as a spoiled, pampered co-
quette who added Jefferson to her salon of admirers.
Others have said it was a romantic friendship filled
with flirtation but no physical consummation. And yet
others have sensed a passion between the two that
never appeared between Jefferson and any other

woman. Given this passion, along with Maria's un-happy marriage and Jefferson's loneliness as a widower, it would not seem unlikely that they consummated their love. The sexual mores of late-eighteenth century France would have been less critical of their relationship than would those of later generations.

Whatever the case, these letters are evidence of a deep and passionate love between Thomas and Maria. Whether consummated or not, it was a relationship that was never resolved. Both people lived long and fruitful lives after their meetings had stopped. But neither ever relinquished the abiding love they had for the other. The phrase from one of Maria's final letters must have rung true to the old farmer as he looked out across his Virginia fields: "Remembrance must be ever green."

"A Day of Contradiction"

{*Paris, Wednesday evening*}, *September 20, 1786*

I HOPE YOU don't always judge by appearances or it would be much to my disadvantage this day, without my deserving it; it has been the day of contradiction, I meant to have had the pleasure of seeing you *Twice,* and I have appeared a Monster for not having sent to know how you was, the *whole day.* I have been more uneasy, than I can express. This morning my husband killed my project, I had proposed to him, by burying himself among pictures and forgetting the hours, though we were near your house coming to see you, we were obliged to turn back, the time being much past that we were to be at St. Cloud* to dine with the Duchess of Kingston; nothing was to hinder us from coming in the evening, but alas! My good intention proved only a disturbance to your neighbors, and just late enough to break the rest of all your servants and perhaps yourself. I came home with the disappointment of not having been able to make my apologies in *propria Persona.* I hope you feel my distress, instead of accusing me, the one I deserve, the other not. We will come to see you tomorrow morning, if nothing happens to prevent it! Oh I wish you was well enough to come to us tomorrow to dinner and stay the evening. I won't tell you what I shall have. Temptations now are too Cruel for your situation. I only mention my wish, if the executing them should be possible, your merit

*A popular resort midway between Paris and Versailles with an extensive park of gardens, statues, and fountains and a restaurant. Louis XVI had recently purchased a château here for Marie Antoinette.

will be greater or my satisfaction the more flattered. I would serve you and help you at dinner, and divert your pain after dinner by good music.—{I don't know why I have written so much in a language which does not belong to me, while I can write in my own, which you understand so well. I did not think of myself otherwise I would not have done so. Anyway, believe me always your most obliged servant and true friend.}

Maria Cosway

"A Painful Night"

Thursday, October 5, 1786

I HAVE PASSED the night in so much pain that I have not closed my eyes. It is with infinite regret therefore that I must relinquish your charming company for that of the surgeon whom I have sent for to examine into the cause of this change. I am in hopes it is only the having rattled a little too freely over the pavement yesterday. If you do not go today I shall still have the pleasure of seeing you again. If you do, god bless you wherever you go. Present me in the most friendly terms to Mr. Cosway, and let me hear of your safe arrival in England. Addio Addio.

[Th: Jefferson]

Let me know if you do not go today.

"Remembering the Charming Days"

I AM VERY, VERY SORRY INDEED, and [blame myself] for having been the cause of your pains in the night; Why would you go? And why was I not more friendly to you and less to myself by preventing your giving me the pleasure of your company? You repeatedly said it would do you no harm, I felt interested and did not insist. We shall go I believe this morning. Nothing seems ready, but Mr. Cosway seems more disposed than I have seen him all this time. I shall write to you from England, it is impossible to be wanting to a person who has been so excessively obliging. I don't attempt to make compliments, they can be none for you, but I beg you will think us sensible to your kindness, and that it will be with infinite pleasure I shall remember the charming days we have past together, and shall long for next spring.

You will make me very happy, if you would send a line *post restante** at Antwerp, that I may know how you are.

*General delivery to be held at the post office.

Believe me dear sir, your most obliged affectionate servant,

Maria Cosway

"Hoping for News"

Antwerp, Monday, October 10, 1786

{I AM ADDING A COUPLE of lines to ask you how you are. I hope the trip to St. Dennys did not cause you to remember us painfully, and that I shall soon receive news of your complete recovery, which will give infinite pleasure to your always obliged and affectionate friend,

Maria Cosway

Mr. Cosway adds his compliments to mine. We arrived here Sunday, three hours past midnight.}

Enclosed as a note added at the end of a letter from John Trumbull to Jefferson written from Antwerp on October 9.

"The Head and
the Heart Converse"

My Dear Madam,

HAVING PERFORMED the last sad office of handing you into your carriage at the Pavillon de St. Denis,* and seen the wheels get actually into motion, I turned on my heel and walked, more dead than alive, to the opposite door, where my own was awaiting me. Mr. Danquerville[+] was missing. He was sought for, found, and dragged downstairs. We were crammed into the carriage, like recruits for the Bastille, and not having soul enough to give orders to the coachman, he presumed Paris our destination, and drove off. After a considerable interval, silence was broke with a "je suis vraiment affligé du depart de ces bons gens."[++] This was the signal for a mutual confession of distress. We began immediately to talk of Mr. and Mrs. Cosway, of their goodness, their talents, their amiability, and though we spoke of nothing else, we seemed hardly to have entered into matter when the coachman announced the rue St. Denis, and that we were opposite Mr. Danquerville's. He insisted on descending there and traversing a short passage to his lodgings. I was carried home. Seated by my fireside, solitary and sad, the following dialogue took place between my Head and my Heart.

Head. Well, friend, you seem to be in a pretty trim.

Heart. I am indeed the most wretched of all earthly beings. Overwhelmed with grief, every fiber of my

One of the magnificent tollhouses on the Farmers General wall surrounding Paris.

[+]*Pierre François Hugues d'Hancarville (1719–1805) had written a work on Etruscan, Greek, and Roman antiquities. Like Jefferson, he was enamored of Maria Cosway. He sometimes served as courier of letters between Jefferson and Cosway.*

[++]*"I am truly grieved by the departure of these good people."*

frame distended beyond its natural powers to bear, I would willingly meet whatever catastrophe should leave me no more to feel or to fear.

Head. These are the eternal consequences of your warmth and precipitation. This is one of the scrapes into which you are ever leading us. You confess your follies indeed: but still you hug and cherish them, and no reformation can be hoped, where there is no repentance.

Heart. Oh my friend! This is no moment to upbraid my foibles. I am rent into fragments by the force of my grief! If you have any balm, pour it into my wounds: if none, do not harrow them by new torments. Spare me in this awful moment! At any other I will attend with patience to your admonitions.

Head. On the contrary I never found that the moment of triumph with you was the moment of attention to my admonitions. While suffering under your follies you may perhaps be made sensible of them, but, the paroxysm over, you fancy it can never return. Harsh therefore as the medicine may be, it is my office to administer it. You will be pleased to remember that when our friend Trumbull* used to be telling us of the merits and talents of these good people, I never ceased whispering to you that we had no occasion for new acquaintance; that the greater their merit and talents,

*John Trumbull (1756–1843), the son of Governor Jonathan Trumbull of Connecticut, had served in the Continental Army as aide-de-camp to George Washington. In 1780, he went to London to study painting with Benjamin West. Trumbull planned to paint the portraits of the leading figures of the Revolution and some of its most important scenes. He met Jefferson in London in 1786.

the more dangerous their friendship to our tranquillity, because the regret at parting would be greater.

Heart. Accordingly, Sir, this acquaintance was not the consequence of my doings. It was one of your projects which threw us in the way of it. It was you, remember, and not I, who desired the meeting, at Legrand & Molinos.[*] I never trouble myself with domes nor arches. The Halle aux bleds[†] might have rotted down before I should have gone to see it. But you, forsooth, who are eternally getting us to sleep with your diagrams and crotchets, must go and examine this wonderful piece of architecture. And when you had seen it, oh! it was the most superb thing on earth! What you had seen there was worth all you had yet seen in Paris! I thought so too. But I meant it of the lady and gentleman to whom we had been presented, and not of a parcel of sticks and chips put together in pens. You then, Sir, and not I, have been the cause of the present distress.

Head. It would have been happy for you if my diagrams and crotchets had gotten you to sleep on that day, as you are pleased to say they eternally do. My visit to Legrand & Molinos had public utility for its object. A market is to be built in Richmond. What a commodious plan is that of Legrand & Molinos: especially if we put on it the noble dome of the Halle aux

[*] *Architects Jacques Guilaume Le Grande and Jacques Molinos.*

[†] *The indoor circular market place on the Right Bank. In 1766 Le Grand & Molinos added a magnificent dome with a wooden skeletal framework and glass panels that allowed light to flood the interior. The dome, the largest in France, was 120 feet in diameter and rose 100 feet.*

bleds. If such a bridge as they showed us can be thrown across the Schuylkill at Philadelphia, the floating bridges taken up,* and the navigation of that river opened, what a copious resource will be added, of wood and provisions, to warm and feed the poor of that city. While I was occupied with these objects, you were dilating with your new acquaintances, and contriving how to prevent a separation from them. Every soul of you had an engagement for the day. Yet all these were to be sacrificed, that you might dine together. Lying messengers were to be dispatched into every quarter of the city with apologies for your breach of engagement. You particularly had the effrontery to send word to the Duchess d'Anville[+] that, in the moment we were setting out to dine with her, dispatches came to hand which required immediate attention. You wanted me to invent a more ingenious excuse; but I knew you were getting into a scrape, and I would have nothing to do with it. Well, after dinner to St. Cloud, from St. Cloud to Ruggieri's,[++] from Ruggieri to Krumfoltz,[‡] and if the day had been as long as a Lapland summer day, you would still have contrived means, among you, to have filled it.

Heart. Oh! my dear friend, how you have revived me by recalling to my mind the transactions of that day! How well I remember them all, and that when I

*The wooden pontoon bridges across the Schuylkill River limited navigation.

[+]*The Duchess d'Anville, a young woman who had been forced into a marriage of convenience with her old uncle.

[++]*A resort park that included a cabaret-like restaurant, an orchestra, and regular displays of fireworks.

[‡]*Johann Baptiste Krumpholtz, a renowned Austrian harpist who had recently designed a new harp.

One of Jefferson's favorite bridges. He referred to it as "the handsomest in the world."

+Jefferson described the royal retreat of Marly as "the most beautifully situated and the most pleasant in all France." It boasted a machine that hydraulically lifted water from the Seine to the plateau and aqueduct for the operation of the many fountains at Versailles and Marley. Occasionally as water was raised a rainbow appeared.

++The château at St. Germaine-en-laye.

came home at night and looked back to the morning, it seemed to have been a month agone. Go on then, like a kind comforter, and paint to me the day we went to St. Germains. How beautiful was every object! the Pont de Neuilly,* the hills along the Seine, the rainbows of the machine of Marly,+ the terrace of St. Germains,++ the château, the gardens, the statues of Marly, the pavilion of Lucienne.‡ Recollect too Madrid, Bagatelle, the King's garden, the Dessert.§ How grand the idea excited by the remains of such a column! The spiral staircase too was beautiful. Every moment was filled with something agreeable. The wheels of time moved on with a rapidity of which those of our carriage gave but a faint idea, and yet in the evening, when one took a retrospect of the day, what a mass of happiness had we travelled over! Retrace all those scenes to me, my good companion, and I will forgive the unkindness with which you were chiding me. The day we went to St. Germains was a little too warm, I think, was not it?

Head. Thou art the most incorrigible of all the beings that ever sinned! I reminded you of the follies of the first day, intending to deduce from thence some useful lessons for you, but instead of listening to these, you kindle at the recollection, you retrace the whole series with a fondness which shows you want nothing but the opportunity to act it over again. I often told

you during its course that you were imprudently en
gaging your affections under circumstances that must
cost you a great deal of pain: that the persons indeed
were of the greatest merit, possessing good sense, good
humor, honest hearts, honest manners, and eminence
in a lovely art: that the lady had moreover qualities
and accomplishments, belonging to her sex, which
might form a chapter apart for her: such as music,
modesty, beauty, and that softness of disposition which
is the ornament of her sex and charm of ours. But that
all these considerations would increase the pang of
separation: that their stay here was to be short: that
you rack our whole system when you are parted from
those you love, complaining that such a separation is
worse than death, inasmuch as this ends our sufferings, whereas that only begins them: and that the separation would in this instance be the more severe as
you would probably never see them again.

Heart. But they told me they would come back again
the next year.

Head. But in the meantime see what you suffer: and
their return too depends on so many circumstances
that if you had a grain of prudence you would not count
upon it. Upon the whole it is improbable and therefore
you should abandon the idea of ever seeing them again.

Heart. May heaven abandon me if I do!

‡*Pavilion de
Musique at
Louveciennes, the
villa built in
1772 by Louis XV.*

§*Here Jefferson
names the
Château de
Madrid, built by
Francis I and a
favorite escape of
Louis XV; the
Bagatelle château
and gardens, built
in 1777 for the
Comte d'Artois,
the brother of
Louis XVI; and
Le Désert de
Retz, the ninety-
acre estate of
François de
Monville on
which de
Monville
constructed an
spectacular house
in the form of a
Roman column.
In the ceneter was
a six-story spiral
staircase.*

Head. Very well. Suppose then they come back. They are to stay here two months, and when these are expired, what is to follow? Perhaps you flatter yourself they may come to America?

Heart. God only knows what is to happen. I see nothing impossible in that supposition, and I see things wonderfully contrived sometimes to make us happy. Where could they find such objects as in America for the exercise of their enchanting art? especially the lady, who paints landscape so inimitably. She wants only subjects worthy of immortality to render her pencil immortal. The Falling spring, the Cascade of Niagara, the Passage of the Potomac thro the Blue mountains, the Natural bridge. It is worth a voyage across the Atlantic to see these objects; much more to paint, and make them, and thereby ourselves, known to all ages. And our own dear Monticello, where has Nature spread so rich a mantle under the eye? mountains, forests, rocks, rivers. With what majesty do we there ride above the storms! How sublime to look down into the workhouse of nature, to see her clouds, hail, snow, rain, thunder, all fabricated at our feet! And the glorious Sun, when rising as if out of a distant water, just gilding the tops of the mountains, and giving life to all nature!—I hope in god no circumstance may ever make either seek an asylum from grief! With what sincere sympathy I would open every cell of my composition to receive the effusion of their woes! I would pour my tears into their wounds: and if a drop of balm could be found at the top of the Cordilleras,* or at the remotest sources of the Missouri, I would go thither myself to seek and to bring it. Deeply practiced in the school of affliction, the human heart knows no joy which I have not lost, no sorrow of which I have not drank! Fortune can present no grief of unknown form to me! Who then can so softly bind up the wound of another as he who has felt the same wound himself? But Heaven forbid they should ever know a sorrow!—Let us turn over another leaf, for this has distracted me.

*Probably a reference to the Andes Mountains.

Head. Well. Let us put this possibility to trial then on another point. When you consider the character which is given of our country by the lying newspapers of London, and their credulous copiers in other countries; when you reflect that all Europe is made to believe we are a lawless banditti, in a state of absolute anarchy, cutting one another's throats, and plundering without distinction, how can you expect that any reasonable creature would venture among us?

Heart. But you and I know that all this is false: that there is not a country on earth where there is greater tranquillity, where the laws are milder, or better obeyed: where everyone is more attentive to his own business, or meddles less with that of others: where strangers are better received, more hospitably treated, and with a more sacred respect.

Head. True, you and I know this, but your friends do not know it.

Heart. But they are sensible people who think for themselves. They will ask of impartial foreigners who have been among us, whether they saw or heard on the spot any instances of anarchy. They will judge too that a people occupied as we are in opening rivers, digging navigable canals, making roads, building public schools, establishing academies, erecting busts and statues to our great men, protecting religious freedom, abolishing sanguinary punishments, reforming and improving our laws in general, they will judge I say for themselves whether these are not the occupations of a people at their ease, whether this is not better evidence of our true state than a London newspaper, hired to lie, and from which no truth can ever be extracted but by reversing everything it says.

Head. I did not begin this lecture my friend with a view to learn from you what America is doing. Let us return then to our point. I wished to make you sensible how imprudent it is to place your affections, without reserve, on objects you must so soon lose, and whose loss when it comes must cost you such severe pangs. Remember the last night. You knew your friends were to leave Paris today. This was enough to throw you into agonies. All night you tossed us from one side of the bed to the other. No sleep, no rest. The poor crippled wrist too, never left one moment in the same position, now up, now down, now here, now there; was it to be wondered at if all its pains returned? The surgeon then was to be called, and to be rated as an ignoramus because he could not divine the cause of this extraordinary change.—In fine, my friend, you must mend your manners. This is not a world to live at random in as you do. To avoid these eternal distresses, to which you are forever exposing us, you must learn to look forward before you take a step which may interest our peace. Everything in this world is matter of calculation. Advance then with caution, the balance in your hand. Put into one scale the pleasures which any object may offer; but put fairly into the other the pains which are to follow, and see which preponderates. The making an acquaintance is not a matter of indifference. When a new one is proposed to you, view it all round. Consider what advantages it presents, and to what inconveniences it may expose you. Do not bite at the bait of pleasure till you know there is no hook beneath it. The art of life is the art of avoiding pain: and he is the best pilot who steers clearest of the rocks and shoals with which it is beset. Pleasure is always before us; but misfortune is at our side: while running after that, this arrests us. The most effectual means of being secure against pain is to retire within ourselves, and to suffice for our own happiness. Those, which depend on ourselves, are the only pleasures a wise man will count on: for nothing is ours which another may deprive us of. Hence the inestimable value of intellectual pleasures. Ever in our power, always leading us to something new, never cloying, we ride, serene and sublime, above the concerns of this mortal world, contemplating truth and nature, matter and motion, the laws which bind up their existence, and that eternal being who made and bound them up by these laws. Let this be our employ. Leave the bustle and tumult of society to those who have not talents to occupy themselves without them. Friendship is but another name for an alliance with the follies and the misfortunes of others. Our own share of miseries is sufficient: why enter then as volunteers into those of another? Is there so little gall poured into our own cup that we must needs help to drink that of our neighbor? A friend dies or leaves us: we feel as if a limb was cut off. He is sick: we must watch over him, and participate of his pains. His fortune is shipwrecked: ours must be laid under contribution. He loses a child, a parent or a partner: we must mourn the loss as if it was our own.

Heart. And what more sublime delight than to mingle tears with one whom the hand of heaven hath smitten! To watch over the bed of sickness, and to beguile its tedious and its painful moments! To share our bread with one to whom misfortune has left none! This world abounds indeed with misery: to lighten its burden we must divide it with one another. But let us now try the virtues of your mathematical balance, and as you have put into one scale the burdens of friendship, let me put its comforts into the other. When languishing then under disease, how grateful is the solace of our friends! How are we penetrated with their assiduities and attentions! How much are we supported by their encouragements and kind offices! When Heaven has taken from us some object of our love, how sweet is it to have a bosom whereon to recline our heads, and into which we may pour the torrent of our tears! Grief, with such a comfort, is almost a luxury! In a life where we are perpetually exposed to want and accident, yours is a wonderful proposition, to insulate ourselves, to retire from all aid, and to wrap ourselves in the mantle of self-sufficiency! For assuredly nobody will care for him who cares for nobody. But friendship is precious not only in the shade but in the sunshine of life: and thanks to a benevolent arrangement of things, the greater part of life is sunshine. I will recur for proof to the days we have lately passed. On these indeed the sun shone brightly! How gay did the face of nature appear! Hills, valleys, châteaux, gardens, rivers, every object wore its liveliest hue! Whence did they borrow it? From the presence of our charming companion. They were pleasing, because she seemed pleased. Alone, the scene would have been dull and insipid: the participation of it with her gave it relish. Let the gloomy monk, sequestered from the world, seek unsocial pleasures in the bottom of his cell! Let the sublimated philosopher grasp visionary happiness while pursuing phantoms dressed in the garb of truth! Their supreme wisdom is supreme folly: and they mistake for happiness the mere absence of pain. Had they ever felt the solid pleasure of one generous spasm of the heart, they would exchange for it all the frigid speculations of their lives, which you have been vaunting in such elevated terms. Believe me then, my friend, that that is a miserable arithmetic which would estimate friendship at nothing, or at less than nothing. Respect for you has induced me to enter into this discussion, and to hear principles uttered which I detest and abjure. Respect for myself now obliges me to recall you into the proper limits of your office. When nature assigned us the same habitation, she gave us over it a divided empire. To you she allotted the field of science, to me that of morals. When the circle is to be squared, or the orbit of a comet to be traced; when the arch of greatest strength, or the solid of least resistance is to be investigated, take you the problem: it is yours: nature has given me no cognizance of it. In like manner in denying to you the feelings of sympathy, of benevolence, of gratitude, of justice, of love, of friendship, she has excluded you from their control. To these she has adapted the mechanism of the heart. Morals were too essential to the happiness of man to be risked on the incertain combinations of the head. She laid their foundation therefore in sentiment, not in science. That she gave to all, as necessary to all: this to a few only, as sufficing with a few. I know indeed that you pretend authority to the sovereign control of our conduct in all its parts: and a respect for your grave saws* and maxims, a desire to do what is right, has sometimes induced me to conform to your counsels. A few facts however which I can readily recall to your memory, will suffice to prove to you that nature has not organized you for our moral direction. When the poor wearied soldier, whom we overtook at Chickahominy† with his pack on his back, begged us to let him get up behind our chariot, you

* *"proverbs"*

† *A small navigable river in Virginia that flows into the James River.*

began to calculate that the road was full of soldiers, and that if all should be taken up our horses would fail in their journey. We drove on therefore. But soon becoming sensible you had made me do wrong, that though we cannot relieve all the distressed we should relieve as many as we can, I turned about to take up the soldier; but he had entered a bye path, and was no more to be found: and from that moment to this I could never find him out to ask his forgiveness. Again, when the poor woman came to ask a charity in Philadelphia, you whispered that she looked like a drunkard, and that half a dollar was enough to give her for the ale-house. Those who want the dispositions to give, easily find reasons why they ought not to give. When I sought her out afterwards, and did what I should have done at first, you know that she employed the money immediately towards placing her child at school. If our country, when pressed with wrongs at the point of the bayonet, had been governed by its heads instead of its hearts, where should we have been now? hanging on a gallows as high as Haman's.* You began to calculate and to compare wealth and numbers: we threw up a few pulsations of our warmest blood: we supplied enthusiasm against wealth and numbers: we put our existence to the hazard, when the hazard seemed against us, and we saved our coun-

*Esther 7:9-10. Haman built a gallows fifty cubits high to execute Mordecai. King Ahesuerus, however, discovered Haman's treachery and had him hanged on this gallows.

try: justifying at the same time the ways of Providence, whose precept is to do always what is right, and leave the issue to him. In short, my friend, as far as my recollection serves me, I do not know that I ever did a good thing on your suggestion, or a dirty one without it. I do forever then disclaim your interference in my province. Fill paper as you please with triangles and squares: try how many ways you can hang and combine them together. I shall never envy nor control your sublime delights. But leave me to decide when and where friendships are to be contracted. You say I contract them at random, so you said the woman at Philadelphia was a drunkard. I receive no one into my esteem till I know they are worthy of it. Wealth, title, office, are no recommendations to my friendship. On the contrary great good qualities are requisite to make amends for their having wealth, title and office. You confess that in the present case I could not have made a worthier choice. You only object that I was so soon to lose them. We are not immortal ourselves, my friend; how can we expect our enjoyments to be so? We have no rose without its thorn; no pleasure without alloy. It is the law of our existence; and we must acquiesce. It is the condition annexed to all our pleasures, not by us who receive, but by him who gives them. True, this condition is pressing cruelly on me at this moment. I feel more fit for death than life. But when I look back on the pleasures of which it is the consequence, I am conscious they were worth the price I am paying. Notwithstanding your endeavors too to damp my hopes, I comfort myself with expectations of their promised return. Hope is sweeter than despair, and they were too good to mean to deceive me. In the summer, said the gentleman; but in the spring, said the lady: and I should love her forever, were it only for that! Know then, my friend, that I have taken these good people into my bosom: that I have lodged them in the warmest cell I could find: that I love them, and will continue to love them thro life: that if fortune should dispose them on one side the globe, and me on the other, my affections shall pervade its whole mass to reach them. Knowing then my determination, attempt not to disturb it. If you can at any time furnish matter for their amusement, it will be the office of a good neighbor to do it. I will in like manner seize any occasion which may offer to do the like good turn for you with Condorcet, Rittenhouse, Madison, La Cretelle,* or any other of those worthy sons of science whom you so justly prize.

I thought this a favorable proposition whereon to rest the issue of the dialogue. So I put an end to it by calling for my nightcap. Methinks I hear you wish to

*Marquis de Condorcet (1743–1794), French philosopher and mathematician. David Rittenhouse (1732–1796), American astronomer. James Madison (1751–1836), Jefferson's close friend and collaborator. Pierre Louis de Lacretelle (1751–1824), French journalist and active leader in the French Revolution.

heaven I had called a little sooner, and so spared you the ennui of such a tedious sermon. I did not interrupt them sooner because I was in a mood for hearing sermons. You too were the subject; and on such a thesis I never think the theme long; not even if I am to write it, and that slowly and awkwardly, as now, with the left hand. But that you may not be discouraged from a correspondence which begins so formidably, I will promise you on my honor that my future letters shall be of a reasonable length. I will even agree to express but half my esteem for you, for fear of cloying you with too full a dose. But, on your part, no curtailing. If your letters are as long as the bible, they will appear short to me. Only let them be brim full of affection. I shall read them with the dispositions with which Arlequin in Les Deux Billets* spelled the words "je t'aime"[+] and wished that the whole alphabet had entered into their composition.

We have had incessant rains since your departure. These make me fear for your health, as well as that you have had an uncomfortable journey. The same cause has prevented me from being able to give you any account of your friends here. This voyage to Fontainbleau will probably send the Count de Moustier[‡] and the Marquise de Brehan to America. Danquerville promised to visit me, but has not done it as

*Jean Pierre Claris de Florian's (1755–1794) one-act comedy Les Deux Billets in which Harlequin struggles with an unscrupulous rival to regain a stolen love letter in exchange for a prize-winning lottery ticket.

[+] "I love you"

[‡] Moustier (1751–1817) was French minister to the United States, February 1788–October 1789. The Marquise de Bréhan was Moustier's sister-in-law and mistress.

*"Chevalier"
Latude was
legendary for his
arrests and
escapes from
prison over a
period of thirty
years.*

yet. De latude* comes sometimes to take family soup with me, and entertains me with anecdotes of his five and thirty years imprisonment. How fertile is the mind of man which can make the Bastille and Dungeon of Vincennes yield interesting anecdotes. You know this was for making four verses on Mme. de Pompadour.† But I think you told me you did not know the verses. They were these.

> *Sans esprit, sans sentiment,*
> *Sans etre belle, ni neuve,*
> *En France on peut avoir le premier amant:*
> *Pompadour en est l'epreuve.‡*

*†Madame de
Pompadour
(1721–1764), as
mistress of Louis
XV, had great
control over the
king's domestic
and foreign
policies from
1745 until her
death.*

I have read the memoir of his three escapes. As to myself my health is good, except my wrist which mends slowly, and my mind which mends not at all, but broods constantly over your departure. The lateness of the season obliges me to decline my journey into the South of France. Present me in the most friendly terms to Mr. Cosway, and receive me into your own recollection with a partiality and a warmth, proportioned, not to my own poor merit, but to the sentiments of sincere affection and esteem with which I have the honor to be, my dear Madam, your most obedient humble servant,

*‡ "Without wit,
without
sentiment,
Without beauty
or youth,
In France one
may have the
greatest lover:
For this
Pompadour is
proof."*

Th: Jefferson

"Better a Little Than None"

MY DEAR MADAM

Just as I had sealed the enclosed I received a letter of a good length, dated Antwerp, with your name at the bottom. I prepared myself for a feast. I read two or three sentences: looked again at the signature to see if I had not mistaken it. It was visibly yours. Read a sentence or two more. *Diable!** Spelled your name distinctly. There was not a letter of it omitted. Began to read again. In fine after reading a little and examining the signature, alternately, half a dozen times, I found that your name was to four lines only instead of four pages. I thank you for the four lines however because they prove you think of me. Little indeed, but better a little than none. To show how much I think of you I send you the enclosed letter of three sheets of paper, being a history of the evening I parted with you. But how expect you should read a letter of three mortal sheets of paper? I will tell you. Divide it into six doses of half a sheet each, and every day, when the toilette begins, take a dose, that is to say, read half a sheet. By this means it will have the only merit its length and dullness can aspire to, that of assisting your *coëffeuse*† to procure you six good naps of sleep. I will even allow you twelve days to get through it, holding you rigorously to one condition only, that is, that at whatever hour you receive this, you do not break the seal of

* "By the Devil!"

† "hairdresser"

** "Happy Days!,"
an aria from
Sacchini's opera
Daranus, which
Jefferson and
Cosway probably
attended two days
before the
Cosways
departed for
Antwerp.*

*† In the places
where she longs
to go.*

the enclosed till the next toilette. Of this injunction I require a sacred execution. I rest it on your friendship, and that in your first letter you tell me honestly whether you have honestly performed it.—I send you the song I promised. Bring me in return its subject, *Jours heureux!** Were I a songster I should sing it all to these words *"Dans ces lieux qu'elle tarde à se rendre"!*† Learn it I pray you, and sing it with feeling. —My right hand presents its devoirs to you, and sees with great indignation the left supplanting it in a correspondence so much valued. You will know the first moment it can resume its rights. The first exercise of them shall be addressed to you, as you had the first essay of its rival. It will yet, however, be many a day. Present my esteem to Mr. Cosway, and believe me to be yours very affectionately,

Th: Jefferson

"One of My First Pleasures"

How I wish I could answer the dialogue! But I honestly think my heart is invisible, and mute, at this moment more than usual it is full or ready to burst with all the variety of sentiments, which a very feeling one is capable of; sensible of my loss at separating from the friends I left at Paris, I have hardly time to indulge a shameless tribute; but my thoughts must be contrasted by the joy of meeting my friends in London. It is an excess which must tear to pieces a human mind, when felt. You seem to be such a master on this subject, that whatever I may say will appear trifling, not well expressed, faintly represented * * * but felt. Your letter could employ me for some time, an hour to consider every word, to every sentence I could write a volume, but I could wish that my selfishness was not reproaching to me, for with difficulty do I find a line but after having admired it, I recollect some part concerns me. Why do you say so many kind things? Why present so many opportunities for my feeling undeserving of them, why not leave me a free consolation in admiring a friend, without the temptation [. . .] to my vanity? I wish your heart [. . .] for it is too good. It expands to the objects he [. . .] too much of his own, and blinds the reality of its demerit. {But what am I doing, that I write so much English when I can write in my own language, and become a little less involved.

I did not know what I was doing, I should like to write it over again. But do I not wish to send you the first sheet, the first lines written upon my arrival in London, let the consequences be what they may? Oh, Sir, if my correspondence equalled yours how perfect it would be! I can only express my gratitude in your friendship. Forgive me if your orders were not obeyed regarding the time allotted me to read your letter. It was one of my first pleasures to find it and I could not resist the desire to read it at once, even at the cost of committing an act of disobedience. Forgive me, the crime merits it. Our voyage was pleasant, my health perfectly restored, the weather good except for those days preceding our departure from Paris, the company of Mr. Trumbull congenial and pleasant. But London, the unpleasant city [. . .] amid the fog and smoke, sadness seems to reign in every heart, if one is to judge from the physiognomies one meets; I must return as soon as possible to my occupations in order not to feel the rigor of the melancholy which is inspired by this unpleasant climate. In the company of agreeable friends, practicing the fine arts a little, one can often avoid sadness, even if something is lacking for perfect happiness. Everything is tranquil, quiet and gloomy, there are no bells ringing to announce to us some festival, service or celebration; even when they call for a

De profundis[*] it is accompanied by the hope that that soul passed to a better life, is enjoying that blessed quiet which the world never grants in full: here at night you hear a voice at every hour which announces to us the fact that it has passed, which reminds us that it will never more return and often leaves us with the mortifying sense that we have *lost* it. There are no monasteries which contain men of God who at all hours pray for us and for all those who do not pray, all who are lost, either in the streets or gambling, in vice and idleness. [. . .] you have begun to write [. . .] your letters will never be long enough, when [. . .] in the long winter evenings there is left some idle moment, sacrifice it to me, to sending me news of yourself. I can hardly wait to receive a letter from your right hand, it must be very inconvenient for you to write with your left. This sacrifice will be received with so much gratitude as, putting faith in the promises made us for good actions, I shall invoke for your reward.

My husband sends you a thousand compliments, I beg you to present ours to Mr. Short,[†] to Monr. D'ancherville when you see him. I shall never forget your attentions to us. Some times we shall mention our contemplated tour next year, either to Paris or to Italy. Many things can prevent its execution, but even greater impossibilities have been carried out. Accept

* Taken from the opening words of Psalms 130 ("From the depths . . ."). This prayer for the dead was traditionally chanted in the Christian liturgy.

† William Short (1759–1849), served as Jefferson's private secretary at the American legation in Paris. Short, whom Jefferson thought of as an adopted son, became U.S. chargé d'affaires in France when Jefferson returned to America in 1789.

Because Jefferson did not know Maria's address, he had sent his head-and-heart letter to her under cover of a letter to John Trumbull.

my best wishes for your health and happiness and believe me your much obliged and affectionate friend.}

Maria Cosway

[P.S.] Mrs. Cosway Pall Mall London—{this address is sufficient}*

"No Patience
to Wait"

{BUT WHAT DOES THIS SILENCE MEAN? I have awaited the post with so much anxiety and lo each time it arrives without bringing me any letters from Paris, I am really worried. I fear lest it be illness or that your arm is worse. I think of a thousand things at once except that my friends should so soon have forgotten me; If you are contemplating making me another big gift of a long letter, I shall beg you to send them to me shorter but more frequent. I no longer have the patience to wait and I am venturing to take up the pen without being sure whether I am to complain, whether I am to re-prove, or whether I am to implore patience, to express my mortification and anxieties of this disappointment, perhaps a letter is en route, in the meantime I shall com-plain because it delays so long in arriving. [. . .] not without [. . .] bring only consequences which often dis-please us, one is wont to think with satisfaction about the excellent qualities of the persons whom we hold in esteem, of our happiness in being able to savor of their value, and to experience the pleasure which a sensitive soul feels in friendship, and what is life, deprived of this sentiment! But when we separate, after the pain of sepa-ration is past, one lives in continual anxiety, one does not receive letters, one imagines a thousand misfortunes, if some mishap occurs one cannot run with succor or comfort, nor receive news of it.

Lord George Gordon (1751–1793) led the opposition to the extension of toleration to Catholics in 1780–1781 that led to widespread rioting. In 1786 he converted to Judaism and attempted to form a financial alliance among Jewish financiers boycotting financial support of wars.

†Royal Princess Amelia, the daughter of George II.

‡John Paradise (1743–1795), an English linguist, and Lucy Ludwell Paradise were part of Maria Cosway's London coterie.

The weather here is very bad, melancholy, and sad. Many of my friends are in the country, so that I spend my time with those few who are here, in painting, playing the harp, the harpsichord, and singing, in this way you will tell me one can only be content. I too approve it, but I don't know there is something so heavy in this air, that all that I do seems to me [. . .] to dissipate my [. . .] although for [. . .] which this climate imposes upon us [. . .] night thoughts, before the fire, and when the imagination is well warmed up, one could go cool off in a river. I do not believe that even the gods would be witnesses to this fantastic performance, so much is the air darkened by the fog and smoke that it prevents the celestial inhabitants from penetrating with their gaze the human foibles of this island.

You will probably have heard of the sensation that Lord G. Gordon* has occasioned recently and of the death of Princess Amelia.† As far as news goes there is no time to send you any, I shall fill another letter with it. When I began this letter I intended to say only three words but unconsciously I have arrived this far without even knowing what I have said, but when women begin talking it is difficult to hold them back, even if they are aware of their saying foolish things.

I have seen Mr. and Mrs. Paradise‡ several times and I often have the pleasure of talking with them of

you. It will always be an infinite satisfaction to mention the name of a person whom I esteem, and this is
felt by your true friend,

I receive in this moment two letters from Paris, but
not from you.}

Maria Cosway

"Transported in a Pocket"

I BEGIN, MY DEAR MADAM, to write a little with the right hand, and you are by promise, as well as by inclination entitled to its first homage. But I write with pain and must be short. This is good news for you; for were the hand able to follow the effusions of the heart, that would cease to write only when this shall cease to beat. My first letter warned you of this danger. I became sensible myself of my transgression and promised to offend no more. Your goodness seems to have induced you to forgive, and even to flatter me. That was a great error. When sins are dear to us we are but too prone to slide into them again. The act of repentance itself is often sweetened with the thought that it clears our account for a repetition of the same sin. The friendly letter I have received from you might have been taken as a release from my promise: but you are saved by a cruel cramp in my hand which admonishes me in every line to condense my thoughts and words.

I made your excuses to Madame de Corny.* She was as uneasy, as you had been, under the appearance of a failure in point of civility and respect. I knew the key to the riddle, and asked her on what day she had returned to town. She said on the 6th of October. I told her you had left it on the 5th. Thus each stands excused in the eye of the other, and she will have the pleasure of seeing you in London. Nothing more will

* *Marguerite-Victoire de Palerne, Madame de Corny, along with Angelica Church, and John Trumbull, made up Jefferson and Maria's "little coterie." Madame de Corny, who had no children of her own, paid special attention to Jefferson's younger daughter Polly and Angelica Church's daughter Kitty, who were close friends.*

72

be necessary, for good people naturally grow together. I wish she could put me into her pocket, when she goes, or you, when she comes back.—Mercy, cramp! that twitch was too much. I am done, I am done.—Adieu ma chere Madame: je ne suis plus à moi. Faites mes compliments à Monsieur Cosway, assurez le de mon amitié, et daignez d'agreer vous meme l'hommage d'un sincere & tendre attachement. Encore adieu.*

[Th: Jefferson]

* *Good bye my dear lady: I am no longer my own master. Convey my greetings to Mr. Cosway, assure him of my friendship, and please accept the homage of a sincere and loving affection. Again, good bye.*

"Anxiously
Awaiting"

{I HAVE TWICE WRITTEN WITHOUT having received a letter from you after the first which I found on my arrival here and which promised me the pleasure of a more frequent correspondence. Every post-day I have waited anxiously. I fear lest your arm be worse, but even that would not prevent your writing me. I take this occasion to send you a couple of lines to ask if you have received my letters, to beg you to send me news of yourself, and to remind you that I am with great esteem, your sincere and affectionate friend.}

Maria Cosway

"Food For My Soul"

Paris, November 29, 1786

MY LETTERS WHICH PASS through the post office either of this country or of England being all opened, I send through that channel only such as are very indifferent in their nature. This is not the character, my dear Madam of those I write to you. The breathings of a pure affection would be profaned by the eye of a commis of the poste. I am obliged then to wait for private conveyances. I wrote to you so long ago as the 19th of this month by a gentleman who was to go to London immediately. But he is not yet gone. Hence the delay of which you express yourself kindly sensible in yours of the 17th instant. Could I write by the post, I should trouble you too often: for I am never happier than when I commit myself into dialogue with you, though it be but in imagination.

Heaven has submitted our being to some unkind laws. When those charming moments were present which I passed with you, they were clouded with the prospect that I was soon to lose you: and now, when I pass the same moments in review, I recollect nothing but the agreeable passages, and they fill me with regret. Thus, present joys are damped by a consciousness that they are passing from us; and past ones are only the subjects of sorrow and regret. I am determined when you come next not to admit the idea that we are ever to part again. But are you to come again?

I dread the answer to this question, and that my poor heart has been duped by the fondness of its wishes. What a triumph for the head! God bless you! May your days be many and filled with sunshine! May your heart glow with warm affections, and all of them be gratified! Write to me often. Write affectionately, and freely, as I do to you. Say many kind things, and say them without reserve. They will be food for my soul. Adieu my dear friend!

[Th: Jefferson]

P.S. No private conveyance occurring I must trust this through the post office, disguising my seal and superscription.

"Wishing Myself With You"

YES, MY DEAR MADAM, I have received your three letters, and I am sure you must have thought hardly of me, when at the date of the last, you had not yet received one from me. But I had written two. The second, by the post, I hope you got about the beginning of this month: the first has been detained by the gentleman who was to have carried it. I suppose you will receive it with this.

I wish they had formed us like the birds of the air, able to fly where we please. I would have exchanged for this many of the boasted preeminencies of man. I was so unlucky when very young, as to read the history of Fortunatus.* He had a cap of such virtues that when he put it on his head, and wished himself anywhere, he was there. I have been all my life sighing for this cap. Yet if I had it, I question if I should use it but once. I should wish myself with you, and not wish myself away again. *En attendant* the cap,† I am always thinking of you. If I cannot be with you in reality, I will in imagination. But you say not a word of coming to Paris. Yet you were to come in the spring, and here is winter. It is time therefore you should be making your arrangements, packing your baggage etc. unless you really mean to disappoint us. If you do, I am determined not to suppose I am never to see you again. I will believe you intend to go to America, to draw the

Thomas Dekker, The Pleasant Comedie of Old Fortunatus *(London, 1600).*

†*While waiting for the cap....*

77

† In 1786 Maria
Cosway composed
a packet of four
Italian songs with
harp accompani-
ment. The first
words that
Jefferson saw
when he looked at
the music made
up the last line of
the song:
"Each sweet
breeze that
blows/ Seems to
say, my beloved is
here,/ I wait, but
he does not
appear."

Natural bridge, the Peaks of Otter etc., that I shall meet you there, and visit with you all those grand scenes. I had rather be deceived, than live without hope. It is so sweet! It makes us ride so smoothly over the roughnesses of life. When clambering a mountain, we always hope the hill we are on is the last. But it is the next, and the next, and still the next.

Think of me much, and warmly. Place me in your breast with those who you love most: and comfort me with your letters. *Addio la mia cara ed amabile amica!**

[Th: Jefferson]

After finishing my letter, the gentleman who brought yours sent me a roll he had overlooked, which contained songs of your composition. I am sure they are charming, and I thank you for them. The first words which met my eye on opening them, are I fear, ominous. "qua l'attendo, e mai non viene."†

"Melancholy
By Nature"

London, January 1, 1787

{ESTEEMED FRIEND,
I have awaited with infinite anxiety the long letter which you announced to me, but I do not know for what crime I must experience the punishment of Tantalus,* every day I believe it near, but that day never comes; in your last letter of a century ago you tell me you have received *one* letter of mine, I have written as many as three of them, as I recall, all directed to the banker according to the address which Mr. Trumbull gave me.† The loss is mine, because it deprives me of those moments which you sacrifice in reading my letters, I recall myself for a few instants to your memory, and it justifies me in the desire which I have to pay you my compliments and to offer you those attentions which you so well deserve through your kindness and friendship for me; and what concerns me still more you do not tell me how you are, whether your arm is cured, whether you have received a book of music which I sent you some time ago. These are subjects enough for you to fill two lines, whose import is of interest only to me and which you may write to please me.—I am the worst person in the world for sending *news* since I never enter upon that subject; I am sensitive to the severity of the season; to this unpleasant climate, and to the melancholy of this country. Perhaps it seems more severe now, after the enjoyable

A mythological king who was punished by being doomed to the lower world to stand in water that always receded when he tried to drink and under branches of fruit that he could never reach.

†On October 13, Jefferson responded to a letter from John Trumbull and enclosed with it his head-and-heart letter to Maria. Jefferson asked Trumbull to help Maria find safe private conveyances for her letters to him.

79

months I spent in Paris where everything is gay. I am very susceptible and everything that surrounds me has great power to influence me. If I am more endowed by nature with any one sense, it is that of melancholy, according to the objects which surround me, it may be dissipated or increased. Such influences affect my susceptibility. I am surrounded by amiable people, friends, and everything that is flattering. I spend most of the time at home and I may say that pleasures come in search of me, because I do not go hunting for them elsewhere. All day I paint, and exercise my fancy on such things as suggest themselves. Great is the pleasure in painting when one is free to follow only when desire is the inspiration. The evening I generally spend in practicing my music, and a charming society makes the harmony perfect. Both unite to produce a truly happy time. I have not been to the opera, but I hear that it is bad, I never go to the theater, and I take more pleasure in *receiving* invitations to engagements than in accepting them. But for what does all this preamble serve, when I began I intended to say only two words, to confess the truth I wish to hold myself to your example; I do not wish to erase what I have written because I am grateful for the pleasure which it has brought me in conversing with you, but I wish to be cruel to myself and punish myself by depriving my-

self of continuing further. I will close by assuring you
that I am always with the same esteem and affection
your most humble servant and true friend.}

M.C.

"An Enfant Gatée"

London February 15, 1787

I HAVE THE PLEASURE of receiving two letters from you, and though they are very short, I must content myself, and lament much for the reason that deprived me of their usual length. I must confess that the beginning of your correspondence has made me an enfant gatée.* I shall never recover to be reasonable in my expectations, and shall feel disappointed whenever your letters are not as long as the first was. Thus you are the occasion of a continual reproaching disposition in me. It is a disagreeable one. It will tease you to a hatred towards me, notwithstanding your partiality you have had for me till now. Nothing disobliges more than a dissatisfied mind, and though my fault is occasioned by yourself you will be the most distant to allow it. I trust that your friendship would wish to see me perfect, and mine to be so, but defects are, or are not, most conspicuous according to the feel we have about the objects which mislead them. We may be apt to feel our own, as to discover them in others, and in both, one of the humane weakness we are subject to. This trait of character, we both possess it, you to compliment me in thought, I for suffering patiently those not bestowed or begrudge them, and silence my pretensions with due consciousness; I feel at present an inclination to make you an endless letter but have not yet determined what subject to begin with. Shall I continue this re-

proaching stile; quote all the what's, and why's, out of
Jeremiah's lamentations, then present you with some
outlines of Job for consolation? Of all the torments,
temptations, and weariness, the female has always been
the principal and most powerful object, and this is to
be the most feared by you at present, from my pen.
Are you to be painted in future ages sitting solitary
and sad, on the beautiful Monticello tormented by the
shadow of a woman who will present you a deformed
rod, twisted and broken, instead of the emblematical
instrument belonging to the Muses, held by Genius,
inspired by wit, from which all that is pleasing, beautiful and happy can be described to entertain, and satisfy a mind capable of investigating every minutia of a
lively imagination and interesting descriptions.—I
have wrote this in memoria of the many pages you
wrote in reply to the scrawls addressed to you by one
who has only a good intention to apologies for such
long insipid chit chat, that follows more the dictates
of her own pleasure, than the feeling of understanding: Allegories are always very far fetched. I don't like
to follow the subject, though I might find something
to explain my ideas. Suppose I turn to relate to you
the debates of Parliament? Was I a good politician I
could entertain you much. What do you think of a famous speech Sheridan has made which lasted five

Warren Hastings (1732–1818) served as governor general of India. The opposition party attacked Hastings' arbitrary rule in India as a means of pulling down William Pitt's ministry. On February 7, 1787, Richard Sheridan (1751–1816) delivered an emotionally-charged speech against Hastings that lasted five hours and forty minutes.

† A reference to Jefferson's Notes on the State of Virginia, begun in 1781 but not published until 1784. This first

(cont.)

hours? which has astonished everybody which has made the subject of conversation and admiration of the whole town. Nothing has been talked of for many days but his speech. The whole House applauded him at the moment. Each member complimented him when they rose, and Pitt made him the highest encomiums. Only poor Mr. Hastings suffered for the power of his eloquence; all went against him, though nothing can be decided yet.* Mr. H. was with Mr. Cosway at the very moment the speech was going on. He seemed perfectly easy, talking on a variety of subjects with great tranquility and cheerfulness. The second day he was the same, but on the third seemed very much affected and agitated. All his friends give him the greatest character of humanity, generosity and feelings, amiable in his manner. He seems in short totally different from the disposition of cruelty they accuse him of. From parliamentary discussions it is time to tell you that I have been reading with great pleasure your description of America.† It is written by *you*, but Nature represents all the scenes to me in reality. Therefore don't take anything on yourself. I must refer to your name to make it the more valuable to me but *she* is your rival, you her usurper. Oh! how I wish myself in those delightful places! Those enchanted grottoes! Those magnificent mountains, rivers, etc. etc. etc.!

Why am I not a man that I could set out immediately and satisfy my curiosity and indulge my sight with wonders!—Since I have been in London there have been a great many little parties. I have attended only a very few of them. I am grown so excessively indolent, that I do not go out for months together. All the morning I paint whatever presents itself most pleasing to me. Sometimes I have beautiful objects to paint from and add historical characters to make them more interesting. Female and infantine beauty is the most perfect object to see. Sometimes I indulge more melancholy subjects. History represents herself sometimes in the horrid, in the grand, the sublime, the sentimental, the pathetic. I attempt, I exercise and end by being witness of my own disappointment and incapacity of executing, the poet, the historian, or my own conceptions of imagination. Thus the mornings are spent regretting they are not longer, to have more time to attempt again in search of better success, or thinking they have been too long and have afforded me many moments of uneasiness, anxiety and a testimony of my not being able to do any thing.—I devote my evenings to music and then I am much visited by the first professors who come very often to play, every evening something new, and all perfect in their different kind. And to add to complete the pleasure a small society of

scientific study of a portion of North America established Jefferson's reputation in America and in Europe as a scientist, historian, and geographer. It examined Virginia's geology, natural history, flora and fauna, human population, agriculture, manufactures, and government.

agreeable friends frequently come to see me. In this manner you see that I am more attached to my home, than going in search of amusement out, where nothing but crowded assemblies, uncomfortable heat, and not the least pleasure in meeting everybody, not being able to enjoy any conversation. The operas are very bad though Rubinelli and Madme. Mosa are the first singers, the dancers are very bad. All this I say from report as I have not been yet.—Pray tell me something about Madme. de Polignac.* They make a great deal about it here. We hardly hear anything else, and the stories are so different from one another that it is impossible to guess the real one. She is expected in England. I send this letter by a gentleman whom I think you will like. He is a Spaniard. I am partial to that nation as I know several that are very agreeable. He is going to Paris secretary of embassy of his court. He has travelled much [. . .]. If I should be happy enough to come again in the Summer to Paris I hope we shall pass many agreeable days. I am in a million fears about it. Mr. Cosway still keeps to his intention, but how many chances from our inclinations to the execution of our will! Poor D'Ancarville has been very ill. I received a very long letter from him appointing himself my *correspondent* at Paris. I know a gentleman who has banished my faith in this occasion for he flattered me with hopes which I have seen fail. However I have accepted his offer. I shall see if I find a second disappointment.

Is it not time to finish my letter? Perhaps I should go on but I must send this to the gentleman who is to take it.

I hope you are quite well by this time, that your hand will tell me so by a line. I must be reasonable, but give me leave to remind you how much pleasure you will give, to remember sometimes with friendship one who will be sensible and grateful of it as is yours sincerely,

Maria Cosway

"Miserable at Losing You"

YOU CONCLUDE, MADAM, from my long silence that I am gone to the other world. Nothing else would have prevented my writing to you so long. I have not thought of you the less. But I took a peep only into Elysium.* I entered it at one door, and came out at another, having seen, as I past, only Turin, Milan, and Genoa. I calculated the hours it would have taken to carry me on to Rome. But they were exactly so many more than I had to spare. Was not this provoking? In thirty hours from Milan I could have been at the espousals of the Doge and Adriatic.† But I am born to lose everything I love. Why were you not with me? So many enchanting scenes which only wanted your pencil to consecrate them to fame. Whenever you go to Italy you must pass at the Col de Tende. You may go in your chariot in full trot from Nice to Turin, as if there were no mountain. But have your pallet and pencil ready: for you will be sure to stop in the passage, at the château de Saorgio. Imagine to yourself, Madam, a castle and village hanging to a cloud in front. On one hand a mountain cloven through to let pass a gurgling stream; on the other a river, over which is thrown a magnificent bridge; the whole formed into a basin, its sides shagged with rocks, olive trees, vines, herds, etc. I insist on your painting it.

How do you do? How have you done? and when are you coming here? If not at all, what did you ever come

A mythical place of complete happiness, i.e., paradise.

†*Jefferson traveled only in northwestern Italy. Here he refers to the Adige River as it flows into the Adriatic Sea at Venice in northeastern Italy.*

for? Only to make people miserable at losing you. Consider that you are but 4 days from Paris. If you come by the way of St. Omers,* which is but two posts further, you will see a new and beautiful country. Come then, my dear Madam, and we will breakfast every day á l'Angloise, hie away to the Desert,† dine under the bowers of Marly, and forget that we are ever to part again. I received, in the moment of my departure your favor of February 15 and long to receive another: but lengthy, warm, and flowing from the heart, as do the sentiments of friendship and esteem with which I have the honor to be, dear Madam, your affectionate friend and servant,

Th: Jefferson

*St. Omer, about thirty miles southwest of Calais, is the closest French port to England.

†Désert de Retz

"It Seems a Dream"

London, July 9, 1787

DO YOU DESERVE a long letter, my dear friend? No, certainly not, and to avoid temptation, I take a small sheet of paper.* Conversing with you would break on any resolution. I am determined to prevent it.

How long you like to keep your friends in anxiety! How many months was you without writing to me? And you felt no remorse?—I was glad to know you was well, sure of your being much engaged and diverted, and had only to lament I was not a castle hanging to [a] cloud, a stream, a village, a stone on the pavement of Turin, Milan, and Genoa etc. etc. No! I entered in the calculation of hours that prevented you from visiting Rome. I am not sure if I had any share in the *provoking part*; oh! if I had been a shadow of this *Elysium* of yours! how you would have been tormented! I must excuse you a little, since you tell me you thought of me, and Italy was your object. You advise me to go [on] this beautiful tour, do you forget, {that it was my cradle, that by the limpid current of the Arno I received life! That my first voyage was to the Tiber. That Turin stopped me on my way to London! With all that I wish you had given me a longer account of your voyage; your observations pleased me, your taste is good, your letters interest me, and I expected almost by right, that you would write me as many pages as you were

In a letter to John Trumbull written on July 16, Jefferson sent his love to Maria and jokingly asked Trumbull to "tell her I will send her a supply of larger paper."

90

days absent. Especially having so many subjects to aid what was lacking in your imagination, it would render writing to me more pleasant for you while you reviewed with your pen those places which gave you so much pleasure. I am truly mortified. Nothing could pacify me, except that these lines are yours, and then I do not measure the sparseness of the lines but the pleasure which they bring me.

I do not know that we shall come to Paris this year. I fear not. My husband begins to doubt it, just at the time when one should begin to prepare to leave. You cannot believe how much this uncertainty displeases me, when I have everything to fear against my desire. Why promise? Why lead me to hope? It seems a dream to have been there and I now wish it to be real, because of the impression it left upon me. At least console me by receiving news of a place which so much interests me. Tell me what comedies there are that are new and good, what operas, what works of art etc. etc. everything that can induce you to write me long letters. You spoiled me in the beginning of our correspondence, I told you, you have not continued.

I have finally had the pleasure of seeing Mdme. de Corny. I like her very much, she is amiable and gracious. I regret not having known her earlier.

* *"well done, very well done"*

† *Abigail Adams (1744–1818), wife of John Adams, U.S. minister to Great Britain.*

You do not tell me anything either of your health or of your arm, *bravo bravissimo.**

I am sorry I have not had occasion to see your daughter who they say is presently here. I do not know Mrs. Adams,† and I flatter myself that if you had believed that I might have been useful to her in any way at all, you would have gratified my desire to show you on every occasion how grateful I am for your friendship for your most affectionate and obedient servant,

Maria Cosway

[P.S.] My husband has the honor to present his respects.}

Will you excuse the liberty I take in troubling you with these letters and a parcel. I shall be much obliged to you if you will be so good to send them. I don't know where the Duchess of Kingston lives as I used to send to her at Calais and have been told she has removed from her house in Paris.

"Feeling the Loss with Displeasure"

Paris, Saturday Evening, December 1, 1787

MY DEAR SIR,

Why will you make such a great dinner? I had told the Princess* of the pleasure I intended myself tomorrow and she seemed very glad to go with me, but had not thought of anybody else; to begin by Mr. d'Hancarville. He is very sorry not to be able to wait on you as he has been particularly engaged for some time past. Mr. St. André[+] I shall see this evening. Monr. Nimscevik[‡] accepts with pleasure your kind invitation. Count Btorki [Potocki] is not here, but I shall deliver to him also your invitation. If my inclination had been your law I should have had the pleasure of seeing you more than I have. I have felt the *loss* with displeasure, but on my return to England when I calculate the time I have been in Paris, I shall not believe it possible. At least if that could soften my regret, I shall encourage my imagination to favor me. Addieu my dear friend, let me beg of you to preserve me that name, I shall endeavor to deserve it: and all the gods will bless us.

[Maria Cosway]

I hope Mr. Short will not be out as his usual when I have the pleasure to come *to you.*

The Franco-Polish Princess Aleksandra Lubomirska, nee Czartoriska, said to be possessed of "beauty superior to any found at Paris and Versailles."

[+] *Jean Bon St. André.*

[‡] *Julian Niemcewicz, Polish patriot and writer who later emigrated to the United States.*

"Avoiding Second Good-Byes"

Paris, Friday night,
December 7, 1787

I CANNOT BREAKFAST with you tomorrow; to bid you adieu once is sufficiently painful, for I leave you with very melancholy ideas. You have given, my dear Sir, all your commissions to Mr. Trumbull, and I have the reflection that I cannot be useful to you; who have rendered me so many civilities.

[Maria Cosway]

"The Pain of Leaving Paris"

London, December 10, 1787

MY DEAR FRIEND,

You promised to come to breakfast with me the morning of my departure, and to accompany me part of the way, did you go? I left Paris with much regret indeed, I could not bear to take leave any more. I was confused and distracted, you must have thought me so when you saw me in the evening; why is it my fortune to find amiable people where I go, and why am I to be obliged to part with them! 'Tis very cruel: I hope our correspondence will be more frequent and punctual than our meetings were while I was in Paris. I suspected the reason, and would not reproach you since I know your objection to company. You are happy you can follow so much your inclinations. I wish I could do the same. I do all I can, but with little success, perhaps I don't know how to go about it.

We have had a very good journey, except the two last days I was very ill. It has been a pleasure to me to find my relations and friends, but it does not lessen the pain of finding myself so far from those of Paris. Accept this short letter this time. I mean to send a much longer one soon, but meanwhile answer me this by a long one. I hope your lovely daughters are well. Remember me to Mr. Short, and believe me ever yours most affectionately,

M. Cosway

"A Little Corner of Your Heart"

** Angelica
Schuyler Church
(b. 1756) was the
daughter of
Philip Schuyler, a
wealthy New
York manor lord,
and the sister-in-
law of Alexander
Hamilton. She
eloped with John
Barker Church,
a wealthy
Englishman.*

How DO YOU DO my dear friend? You came to the invitation of my breakfast the morning of my departure! and what did you think of me? I did it to avoid the last taking leave, I went too early for anybody to see me. I cannot express how miserable I was in leaving Paris. How I regretted not having seen more of you, and I cannot have even the satisfaction to unburden my displeasure of [it] by loading you with reproaches. Your reasons must be sufficient, and my forcing you would have [been] unkind and unfriendly as it would be cruel to pretend on what is totally disagreeable to you. Another reason keeps ever since I am perfectly sure t'was my fault but my misfortune, and then we can bear to be contradicted in our wishes with more resignation.

Have you seen yet the lovely Mrs. Church?* You must have seen her by this time: what do you think of her? She calls me her sister. I call her my dearest sister. If I did not love her so much I should fear her rivalship, but no I give you free permission to love her with all your heart, and I shall feel happy if I think you keep me in a little corner of it, when you admit her even to being Queen.—I have not received any letter from you. I feel the loss of it. Make it up by sending me very long ones and tell me all you do, how you pass your time. When you are at your Hermitage,[†] all

*† A boardinghouse
and gentleman's
club that Jefferson
regularly visited
outside of Paris
sometimes*

that regards you will be interesting to me. Have you
seen any of the gentlemen who I had the honor to in-
troduce to you and who received so politely. The Abbè
Piatolli is a worthy Man, Mr. Niemicewiz a very amiable gentleman [. . .] the Prince Charteressi worthy
of [. . .] manners customs and principles you [. . .]
improve him in all he has so far [. . .] natural disposition and talent!

Again I request write to me. [. . .] My best compliments to Mr. Short and believe dear sir, yours most
affectionately,

Maria Cosway

"Think of Me Often and Warmly, As I Do of You"

Paris, January 31, 1788

I WENT TO BREAKFAST with you according to promise, and you had gone off at 5 o'clock in the morning. This spared me indeed the pain of parting, but it deprives me of the comfort of recollecting that pain. Your departure was the signal of distress to your friends. You know the accident which so long confined the Princess to her room. Madame de Corny too was immediately thrown into great alarm for the life of her husband. After being long at death's door he is reviving. Mrs. Church seemed to come to participate of the distress of her friend instead of the pleasures of Paris. I never saw her before: but I find in her all the good the world has given her credit for. I do not wonder at your fondness for each other. I have seen too little of her, as I did of you. But in your case it was not my fault, unless it be a fault to love my friends so dearly as to wish to enjoy their company in the only way it yields enjoyment, that is, *en petite comité.** You make everybody love you. You are sought and surrounded therefore by all. Your mere domestic cortege was so numerous, *et si imposante,*⁺ that one could not approach you quite at their ease. Nor could you so unpremeditately mount into the phaeton and hie away to the Bois de Boulogne,[‡] St. Cloud, Marly, St. Germains etc. Add to this the distance at which you were placed from me. When you come again, you must be nearer, and move more ex-

**in a small company*

⁺*and so imposing*

[‡]*A beautiful park with paths lined with trees, musicians, and food vendors.*

tempore. You complain, my dear Madam, of my not writing to you, and you have the appearance of cause for complaint. But I have been above a month looking out for a private conveyance, without being able to find one, and you know the infidelity of the post office. Sometimes they mislay letters to pocket the frank-money: and always they open those of people in office. As if your friendship and mine could be interesting to government! As if, instead of the effusions of a sincere esteem, we would fill our letters with the miserable trash called state secrets!—I am flattered by your attention to me in the affair of the tea vase. I like perfectly the form of the one Mrs. Church brought. But Mr. Trumbull and myself have seen one made for the Count de Moustier, wherein the spout is suppressed, and the water made to issue at a pretty little ornament. When he returns he will explain this to you, and try to get me a vase of the size and form of Mrs. Church's, but with this improvement. In this business I shall beg leave to associate your taste with his. Present my compliments to Mr. Cosway. I am obliged to trust this letter through the post office, as I see no immediate chance of a private conveyance. Adieu, my dear Madam; think of me often and warmly, as I do of you.

[Th: Jefferson]

"Still Angry"

London, March 6, 1788

I HAVE WAITED SOME time to try if I could recover my usual peace with you, but I find it is impossible yet, therefore must address myself to you still *angry*. Your long silence is impardonable, but what is the name I must give to ——— Mr. Trumbull and Mrs. Church not bringing me a letter from you? No, my war against you is of such a nature that I cannot even find terms to express it. Yet I will not be in your debt. I think it a great one since it is to acknowledge *one* letter from you, *One* and *short*, however I believe that really you know how I value every line which comes from you, why will you add scarcity? But I begin to run on and my intention was only to say, *nothing*, send a blank paper; as a lady in a passion is not fit for anything. What shall you do when you will be much farther, I can't bare the idea.—Will you give Mr. Trumbull leave to make a copy of a certain portrait he painted at Paris? It is a person who hates you that requests this favor. If you want private conveyance to send me a letter there are many. Ask Abbe Piattoli, Madme. de Corney, and many others. Though I am angry I can hardly end my letter. Remember, I do you justice by not thinking of you now. —

[Maria Cosway]

"In Affection, You Are Greatly My Debtor"

I ARRIVED HERE, my dear friend, the last night, and in a bushel of letters presented me by way of reception, I saw that one was of your handwriting. It is the only one I have yet opened, and I answer it before I open another. I do not think I was in arrears in our epistolary account when I left Paris. In affection I am sure you were greatly my debtor. I often determined during my journey to write to you: but sometimes the fatigue of exercise, and sometimes a fatigued attention hindered me. At Dusseldorf I wished for you much. I surely never saw so precious a collection of paintings. Above all things those of Van der Werff* affected me the most. His picture of Sarah delivering Hagar to Abraham is delicious. I would have agreed to have been Abraham though the consequence would have been that I should have been dead five or six thousand years. Carlo Dolce+ became also a violent favorite. I am so little of a connoisseur that I preferred the works of these two authors to the old faded red things of Rubens.‡ I am but a son of nature, loving what I see and feel, without being able to give a reason, nor caring much whether there be one. At Heidelberg I wished for you too. In fact I led you by the hand through the whole garden. I was struck with the resemblance of this scene to that of Vaucluse as seen from what is called the château of Petrarch.++ Nature has formed

*Adriaen Van der Werff (1659–1722), Dutch baroque painter of Biblical, mythological, and genre scenes.

+Carlo Dolce (1616–1686), Florentine painter known chiefly for small religious canvases and portraits.

‡Peter Paul Rubens (1577–1640), Flemish painter.

++The Fountain of Vaucluse was a natural spring with water issuing from the base of a low mountain near the Sorgue River close to Aix in southern France. (cont.)

On a cliff overlooking the fountain stood ruins called by local inhabitants the Château of Petrarch and Madame Laura.

*Laurence Sterne (1713–1768), British novelist. Jefferson refers to Sterne's satire about a stranger (Diego) with a gigantic nose who arrives in Strasbourg and "turned the city upside down" as the inhabitants became obsessed over the size of his nose. Maria Cosway appears not to have understood the sexual innuendo that Sterne intended and that Jefferson tried to express.

†conversant

both on the same sketch, but she has filled up that of Heidelberg with a bolder hand. The river is larger, the mountains more majestic and better clothed. Art too has seconded her views. The château of Petrarch is the ruin of a modest country house, that of Heidelbourg would stand well along side the pyramids of Egypt. It is certainly the most magnificent ruin after those left us by the ancients. At Strasbourg I sat down to write to you. But for my soul I could think of nothing at Strasbourg but the promontory of noses, of Diego, of Slawkenburgius his historian, and the procession of the Strasburgers to meet the man with the nose. Had I written to you from thence it would have been a continuation of Sterne upon noses,* and I knew that nature had not formed me for a continuator of Sterne: so I let it alone till I came here and received your angry letter. It is a proof of your esteem, but I love better to have soft testimonials of it. You must therefore now write me a letter teeming with affection; such as I feel for you. So much I have no right to ask.—Being but just arrived I am not *au fait*† of the small news respecting your acquaintance here. I know only that the Princess Lubomirski is still here, and that she has taken the house that was M. de Simoulin's. When you come again therefore you will be somewhat nearer to me, but not near enough: and still surrounded by a numerous cortege, so that I shall see you only by scraps as I did when you were here last. The time before we were half days, and whole days together, and I found this too little. Adieu! God bless you!

Your's affectionately,

Th: Jefferson

"Addressing a Stranger—
Longing to Return"

London, April 29, 1788

AT LAST I RECEIVE a letter from you, am I to be angry or not? I think when we go to question and doubt it is a good sing, though I don't know whether it is in favor of you or the manner in which you apologize. Many contradictions will make me answer article by article your letter. My hand for writing made you open my letter in preference to all the others you received on your arrival. I am not obliged *to you* for this distinction. Sympathy, and remorse have my acknowledgements. Afterwards let me tell you I am not your debtor in the least. The fatigue of your journey, the different occupations the &, &, &, & prevented your writing, I agree, but how could you lead me by the hand all the way, think of me, have many things to say, and not find one word to write, *but on Noses?* No, this I cannot put up with, it is too bad, and what is worse it is not indolence, it is what I must add to my misfortunes, and I never thought your name was to be on *that* list. You say my letter was angry. You acknowledge it is a proof of esteem, but you prefer softer testimonies of it. Give me the example if you please. Am I to address a stranger in such confidential terms? who writes to me so short and scarce as possible? Oh I wish my dear friend I could announce to you our return to Paris! I am afraid to question My Lord and Master on this

subject; he may not think or like to refuse, and a disappointed promise of this kind would be too cruel to me.
I cannot bear it. I should be doubly miserable all the
summer; but why don't you come? Your friend Mr. de
la Luzerne* is here, Mrs. Church, we should go to see
many beautiful villas, enjoy all the best England can
afford and make the rest up with our own society; we
shall not have a numerous cortege, I promise to make
myself and my society according to your own wish.
At home we may do it better, if I come to Paris I may
do more what I please this time. There are but four
people I could wish to pass all my time with. Is this
too great a number? when *you* are one, even if you don't
guess the others I am sure you would not object to. I
long to return. I left a bad impression in the atmo-
sphere. I was worse than myself, and really so bad that
sometimes I hardly knew myself. I am much better
now, and my constant occupations for these three
months past keep me in better health or they keep me
in better spirits, and that is the most dangerous malady
I can have. If you want to hear what Italian singing is,
come to London. Marchesi† is here and the most wonderful singer I ever heard. The opera is good but for
want of equal performers with him it is rather dull as
the whole spectacle depending on one person, makes

*Chevelier de la Luzerne (1741–1791) was the popular French minister to the United States, 1779–1784, and to Great Britain, 1788–1791.

†Luigi Marchesi was an Italian castrato singer. Maria Cosway left her husband and child in September 1790 accompanying Marchesi to Italy. She returned in 1794.

the rest appear tiresome. We shall have a new one very soon and wonders are expected.

I cannot announce the portrait of a friend of mine in my study yet, Trumbull puts me out of all patience. I always thought painting slow work, 'tis dreadful now.

How is Mr. Short? Pray remember me to him in the kindest manner, the beauty he lost his heart by is here keeling everybody with her bewitching eyes.[*]

Short and Alexandrine Charlotte de Rohan-Chalot, the beautiful, young wife of the Duc de la Rochefoucauld, had fallen in love with each other.

Say many things to Madme. de Corney. I love her very much and I will add that word to her husband too. When you see anybody I know speak of me if they are agreeable t'will improve the subject, if they love me I shall be recalled to your remembrance with partiality. I would wish to deserve and nourish the good opinion you have of me from your own sentiments, enforce it by those you esteem, and oblige you from a return of the affection and friendship I feel for you to allow without bounds you will always be deficient to

Maria Cosway

Mr. Cosway presents his Compliments.

"A Spontaneous Inclination"

London, June 23, 1788

I WILL WRITE TWO WORDS, to show you I can write *if I please* but as I don't please I shall say no more, as I wait to hear from you. If my silence is of consequence, you will easily be sensible that yours is very much so with me, but I must have patience, oh I break my first intention.

So addio —

M. Cosway

Should I have wrote so much if Mr. Trumbull had not come to ask me to send a letter by a person who is going to see you? Ask yourself if you deserve it? Or if it is not only a spontaneous inclination, or irrestibility to this temptation, though you neglect me, I force myself to your recollection.

"Maria In Waiting"

London, July 15, 1788

Is IT POSSIBLE that I write another letter before I have my answer from my two last! What can be the reason? It is either obstinacy, or constancy in me: but what does your silence mean my dear friend! It seems that opportunities absolutely force themselves on you to recall me to your remembrances, should I have otherwise so much courage or should I be so bold as to *insist* in a correspondence! Mr. St. André is coming to Paris and asks me particularly for a letter to you, when I think of you I forget all formality I only remember your kindness, your friendship. You cannot change; it is only by chance (and this is seldom) if I don't think of you that I suppose I could not write to anybody that does not think of me; then a string of *punctellios* and *formalités* stand frowning before me waiting for the happy time, which brings me letters to answer. Such is the situation of your most affectionate,

Maria Cosway in waiting.

"Love Me Much and Love Me Always"

Paris, July 27, 1788

HAIL, DEAR FRIEND OF MINE! for I am never so happy as when business, smoothing her magisterial brow, says "I give you an hour to converse with your friends." And with none do I converse more fondly than with my good Maria: not her under the poplar, with the dog and string at her girdle:* but the Maria who makes the Hours† her own, who teaches them to dance for us in so charming a round, and lets us think of nothing but her who renders them *si gracieuses*.‡ Your Hours, my dear friend, are no longer your own. Everybody now demands them; and were it possible for me to want a memorandum of you, it is presented me in every street of Paris. Come then to see what triumph time is giving you. Come and see everybody stopping to admire the Hours, suspended against the walls of the Quai des Augustins, the Boulevards, the Palais royal etc. etc. with a "Maria Cosway *delint*."†† at the bottom. But you triumph everywhere; so, if you come here, it will be, not to see your triumphs but your friends, and to make them happy with your presence. Indeed we wish much for you. Society here is become more gloomy than usual. The civil dissensions, though they have yet cost no blood and will I hope cost none, still render conversation serious, and society contentious. How gladly would I take refuge every day in your coterie. Your benevolence, embracing all parties, disarms

*Jefferson refers to a scene from Laurence Sterne's Tristram Shandy, *in which Maria, a beautiful, young woman forsaken by her lover, sits in melancholy beneath a tree with her dog on a leash.*

†*In 1783 Maria Cosway exhibited her lush painting of dancers, "The Hours Crowning Love," to a mixed reception by the critics. The engraving became popular on the Continent.*

‡*so pleasing*

††*delineavit, i.e., drawn by*

"hairdresser"

†*Jefferson refers to two fables: the father gave his sons a bundle of rods to break. After they tried unsuccessfully to break the bundle, the father broke each rod separately— demonstrating the sons' strength in unity. In the second story, a nation of frogs asked the god Jupiter for a king. Looking after the frogs' interest, the god threw a log into their pond. Unsatisfied with the log's complaisancy the frogs requested a more energetic monarch. Jupiter sent the bird who proceeded to eat all the frogs.*

the party-dispositions of your friends, and makes of yours an asylum for tranquility. We are told you are becoming more recluse. This is a proof the more of your taste. A great deal of love given to a few, is better than a little to many. Besides, the world will derive greater benefit from your talents, as these will be less called off from their objects by numerous visits. I remember that when under the hands of your *Coëffeuse,*° you used to amuse yourself with your pencil. Take then, some of these days, when fancy bites and the Coeffeuse is busy, a little visiting card, and crayon on it something for me. What shall it be? Cupid leading the lion by a thread? or Minerva clipping his wings? Or shall it be political? The father, for instance, giving the bunch of rods to his children to break, or Jupiter sending to the frogs a kite instead of the log for their king?† Or shall it be something better than all this, a sketch of your own fancy? So that I have something from your hand, it will satisfy me; and it will be the better if of your own imagination. I will put a "Maria Cosway delint." at bottom, and stamp it on my visiting cards, that our names may be together if our persons cannot. Adieu, my dear friend, love me much, and love me always.

Yours affectionately,

Th: Jefferson

"Be to Me What You Have Been"

MY DEAR DEAR FRIEND,

Cease to chide me. It is hard to have been chained to a writing table, drudging over business daily from morning to night ever since my return to Paris. It will be a cruel exaggeration, if I am to lose my friends into the bargain. The only letter of private friendship I wrote on my return, and before entering on business, was to you. The first I wrote after getting through my budget was to you. It had gone off on the morning of the last post, and in the evening of the same day, yours of the 15th was brought here by I know not whom, while I was out. I am incapable of forgetting or neglecting you my dear friend; and I am sure if the comparison could be fairly made of how much I think of you, or you of me, the former scale would greatly preponderate. Of this I have no right to complain, nor do I complain. You esteem me as much as I deserve. If I love you more, it is because you deserve more. Of voluntary faults to you I can never be guilty, and you are too good not to pardon the involuntary. Chide me then no more; be to me what you have been; and give me without measure the comfort of your friendship. *Adieu ma tres chere et excellente amie.**

Th: J.

* *"Good bye, my most dear and excellent friend."*

"A Little Journey for
So Much Pleasure"

Down Place, August 19, 1788

*Down Place was
the country estate
of Angelica
Church.

MANY THANKS MY dear friend for your two letters. Had
I not reason to scold you? Was such a long silence
friendly? And can you wish me not to take notice of
it? No, that would be a mark of too great an indifference. Next to the pleasure of seeing one's friends, is
that of hearing from them. I never think so much of
the distance we are from them, as the length of time
we don't hear from them. I am much flattered by what
you say of my Hours. I am happy you like the idea, and
the author of that subject has every gratification and
recompense by the wish she has inspired you with, of
possessing some of her work. I thank you for giving
me an opportunity of sending you a little souvenir of a
talent that she would wish to possess in a higher degree that the picture might be more deserving of being hung up in the room you inhabit most that she
may be recalled to your remembrance as often as possible. I shall endeavor to find a subject suited to your
taste, you describe several, and all good, I shall see
what I can do from your pointing out your choice. I
am at present in the country therefore it is impossible
to begin immediately an occupation I shall feel most
happy when engaged about it, as I have nothing with
me to paint with, nor any conveyence for it.

Where do you think I am at present? and with
whom? How much we wish for you and think of you

and speak of you. It is the amiable Mrs. Church, you know her, that is enough, and you are capable of feeling the value of this lovely woman.

I have been made very uneasy with the news that you intend to return soon to America, is it true? and is it possible! Oh then I give up the hopes of ever seeing you again; won't you come to pay us a visit first, it is but a little journey for so much pleasure you will procure us, pray let me entreat you to make me this promise. But we have hopes of going to Italy soon, I am doing everything I can, use every argument, to make Mr. Cosway go next year, then my dear friend you should be of the party. Can you resist this proposition! I leave you to consider of it, and write to me very soon. Mr. Cosway desires his best compliments, and Mrs. Church has told me to say many things to you; I recommend myself to be admitted to half she deserves of affection from you, t'will be a good share but never so much as I have for you —

adieu,

[Maria Cosway]

Wish me joy for I possess your picture. Trumbull has procured me the happiness which I shall ever be grateful for.

"The Way Will Ever Be Wrong Which Leads Us Farther Apart"

YOUR FAVOR OF AUGUST THE 19, my very dear friend, is put into my hands this 26th day of September 1788, and I answer it in the same instant to show you there is nothing nearer my heart than to meet all the testimonies of your esteem. It is a strong one that you will occupy yourself for me on such a trifle as a visiting card. But sketch it only with your pencil, my friend, and do not make of it a serious business. This would render me uneasy, because I did not mean such a trespass on your time. A few strokes of your pencil on a card will be enjoyment enough for me.

I am going to America, and you to Italy. The one or the other of us goes the wrong way, for the way will ever be wrong which leads us farther apart. Mine is a journey of duty and of affection. I must deposit my daughters in the bosom of their friends and country. This done, I shall return to my station. My absence may be as short as five months, and certainly not longer than nine. How long my subsequent stay here may be I cannot tell. It would certainly be the longer had I a single friend here like yourself.—In going to Italy, be sure to cross the Alps at the Col de Tende. It is the best pass, because you need never get out of your carriage. It is practicable in seasons when all the other passes are shut up by snow. The roads leading to and from it are as fine as can possibly be, and you will see the castle of Saorgio. Take a good day for that part of your journey, and when you shall have sketched it in your portefeuille, and copied it more at leisure for yourself, tear out the leaf and send it to me. But why go to Italy? You have seen it, all the world has seen it, and ransacked it thousands of times. Rather join our good friend Mrs. Church in her trip to America. There you will find original scenes, scenes worthy of your pencil, such as the Natural bridge or the Falls of Niagara. Or participate with Trumbull [in] the historical events of that country. These will have the double merit of being new, and of coming from you. I should find excuses for being sometimes of your parties. Think of this, my dear friend, mature the project with Mrs. Church, and let us all embark together at Havre. *Adieu ma tres chere et excellente amie.**

*Good bye my most dear and excellent friend.

Yours affectionately,

Th: J.

"Envious of Those Who Converse With You"

MY DEAR FRIEND,

Give me leave to present you Mrs. Cowley the first female dramatic author in this country, she has most distinguished talents, she is the most elegant writer, great poet, and a great genius, a particular friend of mine and an amiable woman.* You have I hope some friendship for me, speak of me with Mrs. Cowley. You will like her, take care of your heart, she may run away with it. How I envy her and every body that can converse with you. Pray write, pray write, pray write, and don't go to America without coming to England.

God bless you and believe me your most affectionate friend,

M.C.

*Hannah Cowley (1743–1809) was a prominent playwright. Beginning in 1776, she had a play performed almost annually at Drury Lane or Covent Garden for the next twenty years. In 1780 her first book of poetry was published.

"A Little Corner
in Your Affection"

Paris, January 14, 1789

FEARING, MY DEAR Madam, that I might not be able to
write to you by this occasion, I had charged my friend
Trumbull to lay my homage at your feet. But this is an
office I would always choose to perform myself. It is
very long since I have heard from you: though I have
no right to complain, as it is long since I wrote to you.
A great deal of business, and some tribulation must be
my excuse. I have for two months past had a very sick
family, and have not as yet a tranquil mind on that
score. How have you weathered this rigorous season,
my dear friend? Surely it was never so cold before. To
me who am an animal of a warm climate, a mere oran-
gutan, it has been a severe trial. Yet we have been generally cheered by the presence of the sun, of whose
bright company at least you have been deprived. The
weather has cut off communication between friends
and acquaintances here. I have seen the Princess
Lubomirski but once since her return, and Dancar-
ville not this age. So that I am not able to give you any
account of them. But they being more punctual corre-
spondents than myself, have, I expect, given you an
account of themselves. It is some time since I heard
from Mde. de Brehan, and am sorry to tell you that by
what I have heard she is furiously displeased with
America. Her love of simplicity, and her wish to find it
had made her fancy she was going to Arcadia,* in spite

*An ancient
pastoral district
on the Pelopon-
nesus penisula of
Greece.

of all my warnings to the contrary. My last letter from Mr. Short was dated at Rome. The poetical ground he was treading had almost filled him also with the god. Have you arranged all things for the voyage with Mrs. Church? We are so apt to believe what we wish that I almost believe I shall meet you in America, and that we shall make together the tour of the curiosities of that country. Be this as it may, let us be together in spirit. Preserve for me always a little corner in your affection in exchange for the spacious part you occupy in mine. *Adieu ma chere et tres chere amie!**

    Yours respectfully and affectionately,

Th: J.

"Good bye, my dear and very dear friend."

"You Say So Much in Few Words"

London, February 6, 1789

I THANK YOU FOR YOUR last letter, my dear friend, it is short, though a long while indeed writing, but you give me such reasons for your silence that I must forgive it, but it is with reluctance. You are going to America, and you think I am going with you. I thank you for the flattering compliment. I deserve it for I shall certainly be with you in spirit. I shall walk through the beautiful scenes you will describe to me by letter; you shall share my envy between Mrs. Church and you, for I envy both excessively for the reciprocal pleasure you will have in one anothers company; and your return when is it to be? Why don't you announce me that, as well as your departure? 'Tis cruel not to do it and you will not absolutely give us any hope of a visit here, how easy you might do it! Why won't you, forget all the objections you may have *contro questo Paese,* and only think of those friends whose happiness you would make by such an effort and sacrifice for them. I agree with you in many things {regarding a thousand objections against the caprices of this nation, I am disgusted by them day to day. Self-interested sentiments, selfishness in politics, with scandal which reigns without the least regard for personages, circumstances, humanity, and right or wrong: you cannot believe in this moment how much has been explained by a number of black and malicious hearts in

against this country

119

the present state of politics; of the things published daily, intrigues, calumnies, and injustices in which all comment as if in a contest to see who can have superiority by force of atrocities, self-interest, and the least one thinks of seems to be the good of the nation. Oh why am I never to achieve my great desire of finding myself in solitude with a small number of friends? That is the only happiness, it lightens a great deal the way to the unhappiness felt in a crowd which one despises and makes longed for solitude full of every pleasure. One lives without knowledge of evil and enjoys the good without disturbance.}

Shall I have the pleasure of hearing from you soon? I complain of the shortness of your letters, but it is only on the first glance on the paper, but when I read, you seem to say so much in few words that I forget the little number of the syllables for the beauty of the expressions and elegant style. But I do wrong to say these things, you will despise me and think me a flatterer. I sent you a letter by Mrs. Cowley I hope you have seen her. How do you like her? Talk of me with her, she is sometimes too partial but she is a friend of mine, a woman of great genius and abilities and I love her and esteem her much. God bless you my good friend. Continue your friendship to your

M.C—

"Your Bosom Calm and
Soft to Me"

Paris, May 21, 1789

I HAVE NOT YET, my dear friend, received my leave of absence, but I expect it hourly, and shall depart almost in the hour of receiving it. My absence will be of about six months. I leave here a scene of tumult and contest. All is politics in this capital. Even love has lost its part in conversation. This is not well, for love is always a consolatory thing. I am going to a country where it is felt in its sublimest degree. In great cities it is distracted by the variety of objects. Friendship perhaps suffers there also from the same cause but I am determined to except from this your friendship for me, and to believe it distracted by neither time, distance, nor object. When wafting on the bosom of the ocean I shall pray it to be as calm and smooth as yours to me. What shall I say for you to our friend Mrs. Church? I shall see her assuredly, perhaps return with her. We shall talk a great deal of you. In fact you ought to have gone with her. We would have travelled a great deal together, we would have intruded our opinions into the choice of objects for your pencil and returned fraught with treasures of art, science and sentiment. Adieu, my very dear friend. Be our affections unchangeable, and if our little history is to last beyond the grave, be the longest chapter in it that which shall record their purity, warmth and duration.

[Th: Jefferson]

"Feeding on Your Friendship"

Paris, July 25, 1789

MY LETTER OF MAY 21, my dear Madam, was the last I expected to have written you on this side the Atlantic for the present year. Reasons, which I cannot divine, have prevented my yet receiving my *Congé.** In the meantime we have been here in the midst of tumult and violence. The cutting off heads is become so much *á la mode,†* that one is apt to feel of a morning whether their own is on their shoulders. Whether this work is yet over, depends on their catching more of the fugitives. If no new capture re-excites the spirit of vengeance, we may hope it will soon be at rest, and that order and safety will be reestablished except for a few of the most obnoxious characters. My fortune has been singular, to see in the course of fourteen years two such revolutions as were never before seen. But why should I talk of wars and revolutions to you who are all peace and goodness. Receive then into your peace and grace the bearer hereof Mr. Morris,‡ a countryman and friend of mine of great consideration in his own country, and who deserves to be so everywhere. Peculiarly gifted with fancy and judgment, he will be qualified to taste the beauties of your canvas. The Marquis de la Luzerne, an old and intimate acquaintance of his, will bear witness to you of his merit. But do not let him nestle me out of my place; for I still pretend to have one in your affection, though it is a

*leave of absence

†the fashion

‡Gouverneur Morris (1752–1816), a wealthy New Yorker who served as assistant superintendent of finance under the Articles of Confederation. He was in Europe trying to straighten out the financial affairs of Robert Morris. Gouverneur Morris would eventually replace Jefferson as U.S. minister to France.

long time since you told me so. I must soon begin to scold, if I do not hear from you. In order to be quiet, I persuade myself that you have thought me in, on, or over the Deep. But wherever I am, I feed on your friendship. I therefore need assurances of it in all times and places. Accept in return those which flow cordially from the heart of

Your

Th: Jefferson

"Longing for
a Letter"

I RECEIVE THIS moment your kind letter, by Mr. Morris. I thank you much. I did long most excessively for a letter from you. Mr. Trumbull is coming to Paris. I have only as he will tell you half a moment to say *this* little but I will write a longer letter very soon.

*In the meantime   *En attend** believe me
yours most affectionately,

M.C.

"A Sad Scrawl, Answering Your Charming Letters"

I OWE YOU A letter, for the short one I sent by Mr. Trumbull, has not cleared my debt to you, and not satisfied my pleasure. I wish always to converse longer with you. But when I read your letters they are so well wrote, so full of a thousand pretty things that it is not possible for me to answer such charming letters. I could say many things if my pen could write exactly my sentiments and feelings, but my letters must appear sad scrawls to you. If I could fill them with interesting news at least but I have nothing from this country. There has been an extraordinary anecdote in one of the papers, but 'tis either not believed, or not understood, nobody can make anything of it; a discovery which has been made of a conspiracy against the King, the persons are not named though the number is mentioned being three and the possession of papers that would explain and unfold the whole. It makes a noise, but I suppose that in time we shall know more about it. —

I am quite in love with Mr. Morris. Are all Americans so engaging as those I know? Pray take me to that country. Your description has long made me wish to see it, and the people I know confirm my desire.

I wish in your return to France you would come to England, since you will not in your way to America. 'Tis very cruel of you.—

I wish you would send me some account of their affairs in France. 'Tis so difficult to have true news. We read and hear thousands.

Pray prepare a large parcel for the return of my brother or Mr. Trumbull. They will be safe. Give me leave to present my brother to you.* I cannot speak of him if he deserves to be taken notice by you for I can only speak with all the partiality of an affectionate sister.—

I hear Mr. Short is returned. What does he say of Italy? Pray give my compliments to him.—

Mr. Cosway joins with me in compliments to both.—

Believe always [I shall be]
your most affectionate,

Maria Cosway

George Hadfield, a talented architect, who later came to America hoping to be named first architect of the U.S. Capitol.

"Comfort Me in Going;
Encourage Me Returning"

Paris, September 11, 1789

MY DEAR MADAM

I have been very unfortunate in my endeavors to see more of your brother who was so good as to call on me with your letter. I wrote to ask him to come and dine with me. Unfortunately there was an American in the same hotel whose name had some resemblance to that on the superscription of my letter, and a French porter delivered my note to him instead of your brother. A sickness then confined me a week to my room. The day before yesterday, being the first day on which I could write, I wrote again an invitation to him to come and dine with me. The answer was from the hotel that he had left that, they did not know whether for the country, or for England, so that I am deprived of the opportunity of showing him how much I esteem every man of talents, and particularly every one connected with you. I must pray you to become my apologist to him and the organ of my regrets.— Though neither the day of my departure, nor the vessel by which I go be yet fixed, the necessity of being ready to go at a moment's warning, induces me to scribble you a line of adieu, while it is yet in my power. Preserve for me always, my dear friend, the same sentiments of esteem you have been so good as to entertain for me hitherto. They will comfort me in going, and encourage me returning. Were there a hope of meeting you here on my return the encouragement would be complete. I count certainly to be here in the month of May. It is a charming month, and should tempt you also to travel. By that time too this country will be in perfect freedom and tranquillity, and even without that, you will be free and tranquil everywhere. Adieu my dear friend; protect me with your prayers and quiet me with your affection.

[Th: Jefferson]

"Think of Me Sometimes"

I DID NOT ANSWER your last letter, my dear friend, because I was in doubt whether it would find you at Paris, but now I shall profit of Mr. Trumbull's departure to send you a line to put you in mind of me in those still more distant parts of the globe, where your friends perhaps all your heart and sentiments are. It will be very flattering to me if you think of me some times. I was very near coming to see you when Trumbull told me that you was to be at the Isle of White, but I have been very ill with a most violent cold. The weather is very bad, and every difficulty opposes my desire of surprising you with a visit, but why don't you come. It would be so easy so short, and such pleasure to us. I think I could be angry with you for not coming, but perhaps you cannot. You may have your reasons therefore shall say no more.

I will not take more of your time up now but expect a longer letter when you tell me where to write. I am so ill at present I cannot write more.

Believe always I shall be
your most affectionate,

M. Cosway

"We Think Last of Those We Love Most"

Cowes, England, October 14, 1789

I AM HERE, my dear friend, waiting the arrival of a ship* to take my flight from this side of the Atlantic and as we think last of those we love most, I profit of the latest moment to bid you a short but affectionate adieu. Before this, Trumbull will have left you: but we are more than exchanged by Mrs. Church who will probably be with you in the course of the present month. My daughters are with me and in good health. We have left a turbulent scene, and I wish it may be tranquilized on my return, which I count will be in the month of April. Under present circumstances, aggravated as you will read them in the English papers, we cannot hope to see you in France. But a return of quiet and order may remove that bugbear, and the ensuing spring might give us a meeting at Paris with the first swallow. So be it, my dear friend, and adieu under the hope which springs naturally out of what we wish. Once and again then farewell, remember me and love me.

[Th: Jefferson]

"The Privation of Your Letters"

London, April 6, 1790

I FEAR MY DEAR friend has forgot me; not one line ever since your departure from this part of the world! I have heard of you, though not from you. Don't let my reproaches be too severe for I am willing to think you have been prevented by important reasons. However silence from a person who feels the privation of your letters, would be impossible. The greatest effort I can make is a short letter, not to take up too much of your time but to bring you to recollection an affectionate friend in

Maria Cosway

If ever you see Mr. Trumbull I hope you will speak of me together. I shall be happy to have my name breathed up by the delightful air of your country among the charms of friendship, hospitality and many other qualities it possesses, and which I wish I could admire in *persona* as well as I do at a distance.

"Divided By a Wide Sea"

New York, June 23, 1790

I RECEIVED, MY DEAR FRIEND, your favor of April 6. It gives me a foretaste of the sensations we are to feel in the next world, on the arrival of any new-comer from the circle of friends we have left behind. I am now fixed here, and look back to Europe only on account of that circle. Could it be transferred here, the measure of all I could desire in this world would be filled up, for I have no desire but to enjoy the affections of my heart, which are divided now by a wide sea. You know I always ranted about your bringing your pencil and harp here. They would go well with our groves, our birds, and our sun. Trumbull is painting away but being at Philadelphia I cannot have the solace of talking with him about you. They tell me *que vous allez faire un enfant. Je vous en felicite de tout mon coeur.** This will wean you from your harp and your pencil, by filling your heart with joys still more bewitching. You may make children there, but this is the country to transplant them to. There is no comparison between the sum of happiness enjoyed here and there. All the distractions of your great cities are but feathers in the scale against the domestic enjoyments and rural occupations, and neighborly societies we live amidst here. I summon you then as a mother to come and join us. You must

**"They tell me that you are about to give birth. I congratulate you with all my heart."* Lucy Paradise had written Jefferson on March 2, 1790, that Maria Cosway had given birth to a daughter.

tell me you will, whether you mean it, or no. *En atten-dant je vous aimerai toujours.** Adieu, my Dear Maria,
    Yours affectionately,

Th: Jefferson

*"While waiting, I will always love you."

Locations of the Jefferson–Cosway Letters

Except for one letter that is privately owned, all of the Jefferson–Cosway correspondence is located in three libraries: the Massachusetts Historical Society in Boston, the Library of Congress in Washington, D.C., and the University of Virginia in Charlottesville. In the list that follows, "MC" indicates written by Maria Cosway and "TJ" indicates written by Thomas Jefferson.

LIBRARY OF CONGRESS

1786 October 10 (MC)*
1786 October 12 (TJ)
1786 October 13 (TJ)
1787 December 7 (MC)
1790 June 23 (TJ)
1795 September 8 (TJ)

1801 July 20 (MC)
1803 January 31 (TJ)
1805 October 10 (MC)
1822 July 10 (MC)
1822 October 24 (TJ)

*Written as note at end of letter from John Trumbull to Jefferson, 9 October.

MASSACHUSETTS HISTORICAL SOCIETY

1786 September 20 (MC)
1786 October 5 (MC)
1786 October 30 (MC)
1786 November 17 (MC)
1786 November 27 (MC)
1787 January 1 (MC)
1787 February 15 (MC)
1787 December 10 (MC)
1787 December 25 (MC)
1788 March 6 (MC)
1789 October 9 (MC)

1790 April 6 (MC)
1794 November 13 (MC)
1794 November 24 (MC)
1795 December 4 (MC)
1802 February 25 (MC)
1819 April 7 (MC)
1820 December 27 (TJ)
1821 July 15 (MC)
1823 June 18 (MC)
1824 September 24 (MC)

UNIVERSITY OF VIRGINIA

1786 November 19 (TJ)
1786 November 29 (TJ)
1786 December 24 (TJ)
1787 July 1 (TJ)
1787 July 9 (MC)
1787 December 1 (MC)
1788 January 23 (MC)
1788 January 31 (TJ)
1788 April 24 (TJ)
1788 April 29 (MC)
1788 June 23 (MC)
1788 July 15 (MC)
1788 July 27 (TJ)

1788 July 30 (TJ)
1788 August 19 (MC)
1788 September 26 (TJ)
1788 December 23 (MC)
1789 January 14 (TJ)
1789 February 6 (MC)
1789 May 21 (TJ)
1789 July 25 (TJ)
1789 August 9 (MC)
1789 August 19 (MC)
1789 September 11 (TJ)
1789 October 14 (TJ)

PRIVATELY HELD

* Facsimile in Boyd, Jefferson Papers, Volume 10.

1786 October 5 (TJ)*

Bibliography

Boyd, Julian P. et al., eds. *The Papers of Thomas Jefferson.* Princeton, 1950–.

Bullock, Helen Duprey. *My Head and My Heart: A Little History of Thomas Jefferson and Maria Cosway.* New York, 1945.

Burstein, Andrew. *The Inner Jefferson: Portrait of a Grieving Optimist.* Charlottesville, 1995.

Bush, Alfred L., ed. *The Life Portraits of Thomas Jefferson.* Charlottesville, 1963.

Butterfield, L. H. and H. C. Rice, Jr. "Jefferson's Earliest Note to Maria Cosway with Some New Facts and Conjectures on His Broken Wrist," *William and Mary Quarterly,* 3rd ser., Vol. 5 (1948), 31–32.

Cometti, Elizabeth. "Maria Cosway's Rediscovered Miniature of Jefferson," *William and Mary Quarterly,* 3rd ser., Vol. 9 (1952), 150–55.

Dabney, Virginius. *The Jefferson Scandals: A Rebuttal.* New York, 1981.

Donovan, Frank. *The Women in Their Lives: The Distaff Side of the Founding Fathers.* New York, 1966.

Dumbauld, Edward. *Thomas Jefferson: American Tourist.* Norman, Okla., 1946.

Ellis, Joseph J. *American Sphinx: The Character of Thomas Jefferson.* New York, 1997.

Jackson, Barbara Garvey, ed. *Lieder and Other Songs by Women of the Classic Era.* Volume III *Songs of Anne-*

Louise Brillon de Jouy and Maria Cosway. Fayetteville, Ark., 1994.

Kimball, Marie. *Jefferson: The Scene of Europe, 1784 to 1789.* New York, 1950.

Malone, Dumas. *Jefferson and the Rights of Man.* Volume 2 of the six-volume *Jefferson and His Time.* Boston, 1951.

Rice, Howard C., Jr. *L'Hôtel de Langeac: Thomas Jefferson's Paris Residence, 1785–1789.* Monticello, 1947.

Rice, Howard C., Jr. *Thomas Jefferson's Paris.* Princeton, 1976.

Shackelford, George Green. *Thomas Jefferson's Travels in Europe, 1784–1789.* Baltimore, 1995.

Tansill, Charles Callan. *The Secret Loves of the Founding Fathers. . . .* New York, 1964.